THE ABSOLUTE AND
THE EVENT

ALSO AVAILABLE FROM BLOOMSBURY

The Withholding Power: An Essay on Political Theology, Massimo Cacciari
Unnatural Theology: Religion, Art and Media after the Death of God, Charlie Gere
Heidegger and the Problem of Phenomena, Fredrik Westerlund
Understanding Nietzsche, Understanding Modernism, ed. Brian Pines and Douglas Burnham
The German Idealism Reader: Ideas, Responses and Legacy, ed. Marina F. Bykova
The Schelling Reader, ed. Benjamin Berger and Daniel Whistler (forthcoming)

THE ABSOLUTE AND THE EVENT

Schelling after Heidegger

EMILIO CARLO CORRIERO

TRANSLATED BY
VANESSA DI STEFANO

BLOOMSBURY ACADEMIC
LONDON • NEW YORK • OXFORD • NEW DELHI • SYDNEY

BLOOMSBURY ACADEMIC
Bloomsbury Publishing Plc
50 Bedford Square, London, WC1B 3DP, UK
1385 Broadway, New York, NY 10018, USA
29 Earlsfort Terrace, Dublin 2, Ireland

BLOOMSBURY, BLOOMSBURY ACADEMIC and the Diana logo are trademarks of Bloomsbury Publishing Plc

First published in Great Britain 2020
This paperback edition published in 2021

Copyright © Emilio Carlo Corriero, 2020

Emilio Carlo Corriero has asserted his right under the Copyright, Designs and Patents Act, 1988, to be identified as Author of this work.

For legal purposes the Acknowledgements on p. ix constitute an extension of this copyright page.

Cover design by Charlotte Daniels
Cover image: *Momentum* by Fabio Roncato
Courtesy Collezione Valentina Chiminelli Parolin

All rights reserved. No part of this publication may be reproduced or transmitted in any form or by any means, electronic or mechanical, including photocopying, recording, or any information storage or retrieval system, without prior permission in writing from the publishers.

Bloomsbury Publishing Plc does not have any control over, or responsibility for, any third-party websites referred to or in this book. All internet addresses given in this book were correct at the time of going to press. The author and publisher regret any inconvenience caused if addresses have changed or sites have ceased to exist, but can accept no responsibility for any such changes.

A catalogue record for this book is available from the British Library.

A catalog record for this book is available from the Library of Congress.

ISBN: HB: 978-1-3501-1143-1
PB: 978-1-3502-7915-5
ePDF: 978-1-3501-1168-4
eBook: 978-1-3501-1169-1

Typeset by Deanta Global Publishing Services, Chennai, India

To find out more about our authors and books visit www.bloomsbury.com and sign up for our newsletters.

for Chiara
and our children Mattia and Alice

CONTENTS

Acknowledgements ix

Introduction 1

1 A new beginning for Western philosophy 15
   1 History of an idea 16
     1.1 A historical-philological link 17
     1.2 A theoretical affinity 22
   2 From Heidegger to Schelling, via Nietzsche 26
     2.1 System and freedom 30

2 Heidegger's reading of Schelling 39
   1 *Essentia et existentia* 39
   2 Anxiety and the openness to being 52
   3 The 'metaphysics of evil' and the 'metaphysics of the will': The 1936 course and the 1941 seminar 58
   4 *Un-grund* before the 'history of being': Seminar of 1927/8 65

3 The unyielding excess of Being 81
   1 Will and Being 81
   2 Thinking of the positive 92

4 The positive beyond the presence 105
   1 Being that withdraws from the presence 105
   2 *Un-grund* and *unvordenkliches Seyn* 110
   3 The later Schelling and Aristotle 115

5   Being that can (make happen) Being 127
    1   The *Abgrund* of Nothingness 127
    2   Being as *Physis*? 134
    3   Being and Knowledge: The transitive meaning of Being 140

Notes 155
Bibliography 171
Index 176

ACKNOWLEDGEMENTS

The first chapter partially reproduces my essay *Schelling e Nietzsche. Un percorso teoretico*, while the rest of the book takes up and develops the theses of the last section of my book *Libertà e Conflitto*.

Introduction

The revival of interest in Schelling's philosophy, which has grown in particular in the English-speaking world, has in recent years been usefully and curiously intertwined with both the international debate on 'new realism' and the so-called speculative turn.[1] This is probably rooted in the centrality and radicality of Schelling's 'realism' (or 'overrealism') within the philosophical-rational project of Modernity and German Idealism in particular. This is a realism that can certainly be traced back to his positive philosophy, although understanding of this latter phase of Schelling's speculation can only and inevitably be gained through a preliminary insight into the fundamental theses of his *Naturphilosophie* and thus through the understanding of his particular notion of nature,[2] which for Schelling was the great omission in modern philosophy.[3]

If it is true, as Maurizio Ferraris and Mario De Caro observe,[4] that the real novelty of 'new' realism lies in the fact that it is aware of coming *after* postmodernism in its various manifestations,[5] then the meaning that Schelling's philosophy assumes within it is even further reinforced. Schelling is in fact the mystery of the philosophy of the crisis[6] that follows the rational philosophical project of modernity, in that, on the one hand, he contributed to the construction of the Hegelian system and, on the other, he could therefore show its structural weakness and theoretical unsustainability.

The nihilistic conclusions of postmodernism do not derive, in fact, from the so-called and presumed anti-Hegelian irrationalism highlighted, for example, by Lukács in a reconstruction that sees Schelling himself with his 'intellectual intuition' among the first exponents, rather they derive precisely from the typical idea of post-Kantian correlationalism according to which thought and being are fully converted, to the point of retaining it impossible 'to consider the realms of subjectivity and objectivity independently one of another'.[7] This attempt to reduce being and thought to their correlation is carried out in a masterly way in Hegel's panlogistic system, but encounters, in the postmodern shift, the exasperation of the subjectivation of being, that is, of the idea that being depends on the thought applied to it by the thinking subject, whose interpretation (in fact always relative and partial) becomes paradigmatic for being itself, and that nothing is outside of that interpretation.

Schelling's position, as is well known, goes beyond these conclusions, since already from his, so to speak, *critical-Fichtean* period he shows how being presents itself as irreparably in excess in relation to thought. The incisive thesis of positive philosophy which states 'it is not because there is thinking that there is being, but rather because there is being that there is thinking'[8] finds the theoretical antecedent of reference in the *ontological excess* highlighted with respect to the 'reflection' already in the first years of his speculative path. Here, in Schelling, an 'ancestral',[9] so to speak, concept of Nature matures first in opposition to Fichte and then in contrast to Hegel, which, on the one hand, cannot be relegated to the inert sphere of Fichte's non-Ego and, on the other, cannot coincide with the alienation of the idea that must be overcome and re-included in the Hegelian Concept. Nature is therefore understood by Schelling as an autonomous position (*Setzung*) of self, and as a precondition (*Voraussetzung*) of being in general and of the Ego (and therefore of thought) in particular, according to a definition of nature such as *Physis* that Heidegger takes up and develops in the second phase of his thought, in a particularly clear and effective way in his commentary on Hölderlin's poem, *Wie wenn am Feiertage* (*As When on a Holiday*).

In his critique of correlationalism, appropriately conducted in his *Après la finitude*, Meillassoux even leads the thought of Heidegger's *Ereignis* to a philosophical stance incapable of thinking about the Absolute, inasmuch as it – by definition – should be freed by the correlation between being and thought.[10] This assumption, clearly functional to Meillassoux's discourse, starts from the idea that Heidegger's *Ereignis* can be summed up in the theses set out in *Identity and Difference* (1957), where Heidegger effectively insists on the co-appropriation (*Zusammengehörigkeit*) of 'being' and 'thought' as a distinctive trait of the *Ereignis*, understood precisely as an event of reciprocal appropriation.[11] And yet the *Ereignis* is also and above all a co-appropriation of 'being' and 'time', as can be clearly seen, for example, in the *Zeit und Sein* conference held in 1963, where a fundamental aspect of the *Ereignis* is equally clearly clarified. In fact, what is even more important than the 'accusation' of correlationalism is that Heidegger's *Ereignis* always contains the idea of an excess, described by Heidegger through the notion of *Enteignis* ('expropriation' which always accompanies the 'appropriation' of the *Ereignis*), which prevents one from thinking of being and thought in their full and perfect correlation.

On the other hand, it is precisely the passages of *Identity and Difference* that offer greater legitimization of the theses put forward by Agamben, in an essay from 1982 later published in the collection entitled *Potentialities*, regarding the possibility of Heidegger's *Ereignis* superimposing on and coinciding with Hegel's *Absolute*. Agamben's essay, certainly enlightening on the etymological roots of *Ereignis* and in its general affinity to the Absolute,[12] is, however, incapable of restoring the 'absoluteness' – the aseity – of both the *Ereignis* and the Absolute, seen here precisely exclusively, in a Hegelian sense, as the 'result' of a movement, rather than as an inexhausted and in-it-self origin from which come the various and multiple forms of being.

As an ontological excess that 'occasions' (makes possible, makes happen) being without ever resolving itself completely in thought and forms (manifestations) of being itself, the *Ereignis* is rather to be read in affinity with another form of Absolute, namely with that proposed by Schelling in the early nineteenth century and further clarified in his *Philosophical Investigations into the Essence of Human Nature*: a form of Absolute that, *schlechtin betrachtet*, coincides with the groundlessness of being (*Un-grund*) and with its unprethinkability (or, if you like, 'ancestrality'), that is, with a dynamic that ensures being and its forms (including the thought applied to being) without ever coinciding fully with such manifestations.

Precisely in aligning Heidegger's *Ereignis* with Schelling's Absolute, I think I can highlight the basis for a form of 'positive philosophy' present in Heidegger's second phase, that is, in the thinking that follows *Being and Time* and, after the so-called turn, revolves around the thought of the *Ereignis* as Heidegger himself states in the *Letter on Humanism*.

To speak of 'positive philosophy' with regards to Heidegger's second phase of thought necessarily implies a reflection on what in general is to be understood by the expression, starting with Schelling's philosophical project. We know that Schelling's positive philosophy imposes itself as a philosophical programme, also in opposition to Hegel's theses, starting from the thought about the *Wirklichkeit* (actuality) of being inasmuch as it simply exists. And yet positive philosophy must not be confused with a mere ontic realism that starts from the phenomenological evidence of the existent and is reduced to that evidence. It is rather a thought that intends to think of being *a parte rei*, in its (free) becoming, in its original groundlessness, and which is clarified as a philosophy *of* nature as per an expression where what prevails is the subjective sense of the genitive, that is, an expression of nature itself as a Subject that, among other activities, also has the thought about itself. It goes without saying that this concept of positive philosophy was not immediately accepted. On the wave of criticism of Hegel's concept of *Wirklichkeit*, positive philosophy on a purely theoretical level, and therefore beyond its narrative character linked to the exposition of the phases of mythology and the history of revelation, has been understood as a theoretical assumption of historical materialism and twentieth-century existentialism, in fact betraying the theoretical intent of Schelling's philosophy of existence in both senses.

The juxtaposition suggested by Karl Löwith of Schelling's positive philosophy with Heidegger's early philosophy of existence – a juxtaposition that at first seems to partly confirm our thesis – does not fully encompass the theoretical scope of positive philosophy and does not pick up on the closeness that is instead registered on another level.

According to Löwith, 'the "effectiveness" of existence – inherent in the *factum brutum* of "that-is" – and Heidegger's "being thrown into the world" and "projecting oneself into the future", all correspond to Schelling's "real existent".[13] And yet it is Löwith himself who points out that the Heidegger of *Being and Time* builds a 'system of being-there (*Dasein*)' inspired by Kierkegaard's philosophy of existence, which, however, completely lacks the ontological tension that Schelling highlighted between the negative philosophy of 'reason' and the positive philosophy of 'existence'.

The *ontological excess* highlighted by Schelling stems from a philosophy of existence that cannot be reduced in any way to a *system of Being-there* because it concerns the dynamics of being as a whole, being-there (*Dasein*) and its activities included. On the other hand, after *Being and Time*, Heidegger himself recognizes through the 'turn' that to understand the sense of being one cannot start from a particular entity, even if it is the being-there of man, but must turn directly to the Being. Heidegger is in fact quite clear when, in thinking of the 'other beginning' of thought, which is announced in the turn, he describes philosophy as something that directly concerns being even before man and therefore before thought:

> If philosophy 'is', it is not because there are philosophers, nor are there philosophers because philosophy is discussed, but there is philosophy and there are philosophers when the *truth of being itself becomes its own* [*sich-ereignet*] and in the way in which it becomes its own, and the history of this making itself its own is exempt from all human preparation and planning, since it itself is the first grounding of the possibility of *being* of human history.[14]

This thought does nothing but continue the basic intuition present at the time of *Being and Time*. If the thrown-structure of the *Dasein* is what Heidegger defines there as the *Faktizität* of existence, it in itself still requires as a prerequisite (*Voraussetzung*) a sphere 'from which' it is 'thrown' (*geworfen*) that includes being in its entirety and in its dynamics: and this is exactly the sphere that progressively becomes the 'object' of investigation in a 'positive philosophy' from Heidegger's second phase.

In a first approach the question seems to re-propose the classic problem of metaphysics that thinks of being starting from a grounding: the sphere enlightened by the *Faktizität* of the existence of the *Dasein* can no longer be described in the language of 'metaphysics' that thinks of being starting from its oblivion in favour of the entity. Heidegger therefore begins to describe it, starting with the 1929 conference *Was ist Metaphysik?*, as *Nichts* (nothing): a concept that Walter Schulz already suggested should be read in affinity with Schelling's *Dass* of existence[15] and that in Luigi Pareyson's opinion should also be read in continuity with Schelling's concept of Freedom.[16]

This *Nichts*, which intends to describe the ontological excess never solvable in the intellect in terms that are no longer onto-theological and therefore post-metaphysical, anticipates and accompanies, while remaining in the background, the subsequent notion of *Ereignis* with its inevitable proximity to the notion of *Physis*. In this, the affinity with Schelling's thought clearly emerges, where the actuality of that *ontological excess* is not relegated to a space that is opaque and impenetrable to reason, but rather believes that it should be understood as an inexhaustible 'reserve of being', that is to say, as a *natural* and dynamic sphere within which act the original forces and powers of being that, in their becoming and in their coessential interaction with nothingness (a concept necessary to highlight the contingency of being and therefore its unfounded freedom), determine its various manifestations, including thought.

For Schelling this *ontological excess* coincides with absolute Freedom, which, however, in turn, must not be thought of as a sphere pacified and sutured by the definitive victory of Being over Nothing, or Good over Evil, but as the essential and original conflict between the Nothing of the Beginning and the *necessity* of Being inasmuch as it exists: a conflict which, however, does not take place only at the origin of being, but rather historically (*geschichtlich*) constitutes the very essence of being and the units it produces, and which also reappears in the dynamics that Heidegger intends to describe through the *Ereignis* as the 'figure' of being that exceeds the 'history of being' as metaphysics.

In the 'first beginning' of thought – Heidegger argues in *Fundamental Questions of Philosophy*, a volume that collects the lectures from 1937 to 1938, a period in which the philosopher was also occupied with *Contributions to Philosophy* where the theoretical bases for the thought of *Ereignis* were laid – the Greeks had the task of answering the question of what being was, and they experienced being as *Physis*. However, *Physis* progressively lost its original meaning of 'origin, unfold-impose itself, of unconcealedness (*aletheia*)', to become 'nature' understood as the sum of the entities inasmuch as they are present. For the Greeks originally, *Physis*, as the distinctive character of being, is *aletheia*. In the progressive oblivion of being, the entity is no longer recognized as *Physis*, but as what is grasped and understood (in full 'correlation') as being present and so the question about being ends up preventing the questioning of the *aletheia* of *Physis*, but remains with the thought that thinks of entity inasmuch as it is present: to make the entity appear, the horizon (that is the *Physis* as unconcealedness, *aletheia*) in which the entity appears must somehow be neglected.

In the 'first beginning', the *Grundstimmung* (the fundamental emotional tonality) was the wonder, the amazement (the *thaumazein*): 'a necessity which arose from the entity itself in its totality, in the measure in which the entity had to achieve, in its being-existent, knowledge and be preserved in its truth'.[17] Now, Heidegger says, in the time in which the 'other beginning' is being prepared, 'the necessity that pushes us in this new turn must come again and only from the entity in its totality',[18] that is – we should say – from *Physis* in the original sense assigned to it by the Greeks. In fact, since the question of being that guided the first beginning is necessarily accompanied by the oblivion of being, Heidegger rhetorically asks whether this very abandonment of being is not a make-own (*Ereignis*) that comes from the entity in its totality, that is, is not the 'most hidden and the most proper grounding and essence of what Nietzsche calls "nihilism".[19] For Heidegger, access to the Openness of the *Physis* must come from a necessity, that is, 'from the abandonment of the entity by the being, when we take seriously the fact that the being escapes the entity',[20] that is to say it exceeds it. But it is probable, as Heidegger himself hypothesizes, that the Openness of *Physis* 'is in the first place the clearing, the enlightenment [*Lichtung*] in the middle of the entity, the enlightenment in which the concealing of the being must become evident'.[21] This means that being shows itself as a becoming, as a process in which the oblivion of being is included, as well as the possibility of the 'other beginning': it is a process that, in order to perpetuate itself and to guarantee movement, cannot be fully realized by a definitive appropriation such as, for example, seems to be accomplished in technology as imposition and dominion over being,[22] but rather by an ontological and dynamic excess that is precisely described by the *Physis* of the Greeks – a concept to which Heidegger returns with great clarity in his commentary on Hölderlin's poetic composition *Wie wenn am Feiertage*.

> *Physis, phyein* means growth. But what did the Greeks mean by growth? Not as a quantitative growth, not even as 'evolution', nor as the succession of a 'becoming'. *Physis* is an emerging and an arising, a self-opening, which, while rising, at the same time turns back into what has emerged, and so shrouds within itself that which on each occasion gives presence to what is present. Thought as a fundamental word, *Physis* signifies a rising into the open: the lighting (*das Lichten*) of that clearing (*Lichtung*) into which anything may enter appearing, present itself in its outline, show itself in its 'appearance' (*eidos*, idea) and be present as this or that. *Physis* is that rising-up which goes-back-into-itself; it names the coming to presence of that which dwells in the rising-up and thus comes to presence as open. *Physis* is that rising-up which goes-back-into-itself; it names the coming to presence of that which dwells in the rising-up and thus comes to presence as open.[23]

For Hölderlin – quoted and commented on by Heidegger – *Physis*, nature as chaos that opens and presides over entities, is above the gods: it is the sacred itself. 'Nature is higher than "the" gods. She, "the powerful", is still capable of something other than the gods: as the clearing [*Lichtung*], in her everything can first be present'.[24] Only nature guarantees and preserves within itself the possibility for entities to appear, but since entities appear *by* (through) nature and *in* nature, it cannot serve as a grounding. In this lies its superiority over the gods and God. A philosophy that knows how to think about *Physis* and the becoming of entities in this way is no longer onto-theological, because the grounding (*theos*, God) is, if anything, in the very possibility of *Physis*, and this never depends on that. *Physis*, therefore, as a sacred chaos from which everything comes and where everything happens, seems perfectly capable of exposing that double and mutual appropriation of being and thought and of being and time that the *Ereignis*, in all its various forms, would like to describe. In this sense, it is even more plausible to juxtapose Heidegger's *Ereignis* with Schelling's Absolute: the progressive definition of the latter is based on Schelling's reflections on the philosophy of nature and the philosophy of identity. In Schelling it is evident that the Greek notion of *Physis* is used, on the one hand, obviously, to describe the process and the productivity of being in general and, on the other, to highlight an unfounded and inexhausted origin that guarantees and preserves in the process the entities produced, without, however, ever being reduced to the process itself and its components. What is already described in Schelling's definition of the Absolute in his philosophy of Identity, where he talks of a 'double life' of the entities in the infinite and in the finite, is even more evident in the introduction, in *Philosophical Investigations*, of the *Un-grund* as the absolute absolutely considered (*schlechtin betrachtet*). This introduction further clarifies the affinity of the absolute with the *Physis* described earlier. On the one hand, in fact, the absolute describes the totality of the entities in the process of their becoming and, on the other hand, the absolute, as 'absolutely considered', is freed by the process itself while guaranteeing it as an inexhausted and unfounded dynamic resource.

The double and reciprocal appropriation of 'being-time' and 'being-thought', which describes the (temporal) happening of the entities and the possibility of their understanding, is therefore accompanied by both the notion of the Absolute and the notion of the *Ereignis*, on the condition, however, of thinking of the Absolute in itself as 'freed', 'separated', from the process it describes and from the completed appropriation.

As Giorgio Agamben observes, for Hegel 'the Absolute, originating in a past participle, needs an absolution that ultimately allows it to be only at the end what it truly is'.[25] In this case, understanding therefore the Absolute as the 'result' of a process, the affinity with *Ereignis* is reduced to what has already 'happened' and which can therefore be described as a sign of the absolute correlation between being and thought – and, if anything, to the *necessity* of what will always happen in this perspective of full 'correlation'. However, since the co-appropriation evoked by the *Ereignis* concerns above all the being-time relationship, the absolute cannot merely be resolved in the becoming of the Concept, in its movement, but must remain capable of absolving itself from the process itself, that is, of refraining from the happening (of the entities and forms of thought) that it always ensures. As I believe emerges ever more clearly, the *Ereignis* refers in fact to a dynamic excess that has much to do with the notion of *Physis* mentioned earlier, as well as with the complex definition of Absolute articulated by Schelling in his *Philosophical Investigations* through the introduction of the *Un-grund*. Thus understood, the affinity between the Absolute and the Event is clarified, even in the contemporary debate, as a passage (or a return?) to a non–onto-theological metaphysics.

The central question of the so-called new realism, in which the present reflection on the affinity between Schelling's Absolute and Heidegger's *Ereignis* is also inserted, is certainly a question of a purely ontological nature. However, the reflections that this philosophical movement brings with it seem to attest more to the *ontic* level of the reality of facts and things than to the strictly *ontological* level, and this perhaps in order to respond to the worst praxis of postmodernism, in opposition to which, in fact, 'new realism' is placed.

In order to understand the ontological instance underlying 'new realism', I believe it may be useful to refer to Heidegger's *ontological difference*, thus highlighting how the question posed by Heidegger, also through the complex notion of *Physis*, inevitably and rightly ends up becoming *metaphysical*.

If it is fair to say, through Quine, that ontology is essentially the philosophical discourse that attempts to answer the question 'What is there?', then certainly it is not legitimate to evade the question 'What is being, insomuch as it is?', which immediately follows and indeed, in some ways, is already presumed within it. It is true that this issue is a question of a *metaphysical* nature, but for this very reason I feel it worthy of investigation.

How is it possible to say, in fact, *what there is* without understanding what *being* is and what it means? If we admit that ontology essentially answers the question 'What *is* being, inasmuch as it is?', and on that basis establishes what there actually *is*, we must, then, also consider that the first question must be read in the double meaning of the copula *is*. That is, answering the question 'What *is* being inasmuch as it is?' certainly means clarifying first of all what actually *is* that which *is* insomuch as it is; and through this interpretation of the question we move into the ontic sphere of being. The other interpretation of the question, 'What *is* being inasmuch as it is?' presupposes, instead, a *transitive* reading, so to speak, of the copula: that is, what *is* the being, what *can* the being, what allows the being *to be* what it is? In this truly 'ontological' sense of the question lies the *metaphysical* question, which, as Heidegger observed, runs a not insignificant risk of slipping into onto-theology.

However, precisely in Schelling's Absolute (which anticipates the 'unprethinkable being' of his positive philosophy) and then in Heidegger's *Ereignis*, where in the *giving* of being, as a destinating, the *who-what* of this *giving* always 'abstains' in an indefinable – in fact 'unprethinkable' – *ontological excess*, inasmuch as it poses the ontological question of the being that *is* (in the *transitive* sense) the existent, there is the possibility of an 'other beginning' for thought, the possibility of a *metaphysical* Principle, which escapes the onto-theological concept described and criticized by Heidegger, and yet preserves the *original and ongoing potentiality* of being.

The definition of this Principle, which makes Schelling a *post-Heideggerian* thinker (in the sense that with his positive philosophy he overcomes the limits of the metaphysical thought described and criticized by Heidegger as the history of the oblivion of being), has been found in the ontological Freedom of the Absolute, *in the sense that it is the Conflict itself that precedes the opposition between necessity and freedom*: that is, it is that ineliminable difference that coincides with the *unprethinkable being* and that is described by Schelling (through recourse to Aristotle) in its *pure* contingency, that is opposed 'with necessity' to the *potency* of being, thus realizing the being itself, in whose average understanding we live and act.

Heidegger himself, however, through the notion of *Ereignis*, proposes in fact a form of 'positive philosophy' that heads towards a non–onto-theological *metaphysics*, illuminating in the original *Physis* the possibility of an 'other beginning' of philosophy.

> At the beginning of Being's unconcealment, Being, *einai, eon* is thought, but not the 'It gives', 'there is'. Instead, Parmenides says *esti gar einai*, 'For Being is'. Years ago, in 1947, in the *Letter on Humanism*, I noted with reference to this saying of Parmenides: 'The *esti gar einai* of Parmenides is still unthought today.' This note would like to point out for once that we must not rashly give to the saying 'For Being is' a ready interpretation which makes what is thought in it inaccessible. Anything of which we say 'it is' is thereby represented as a being. But Being is not a being. Thus the *esti* that is emphasized in Parmenides' saying cannot represent the Being which it names as some kind of a being. Translated literally, the *esti* thus emphasized does mean 'it is'. But the emphasis discerns in the *esti* what the Greeks thought even then in the *esti* thus emphasized and which we can paraphrase by: 'It is capable.' However, the meaning of this capability remained just as unthought, then and afterward, as the 'It' which is capable of Being. To be capable of Being means: to yield and give Being. In the *esti* there is concealed the It gives.

> In the beginning of Western thinking, Being is thought, but not the 'It gives' as such. The latter withdraws in favour of the gift which It gives. That gift is thought and conceptualized from then on exclusively as Being with regard to beings.[26]

Heidegger points out that in the 'history of being' Western thought neglected the It that gives (the *Es* of *Es gibt*) in favour of the *gift* (the being inasmuch as it is present) that the It gives. The *Es* cannot, however, be thought of as it is in the language of onto-theological metaphysics, since the *Es* of the *Es gibt* is similar to the original *Physis*, that is to the Indifference of the *Un-grund*, to the plainly thought Absolute, and to the *unvordenkliches Seyn* (the 'purely contingen') of Schelling's positive philosophy, and all this can be said only in the 'giving', in the 'make happen', in the 'to destine'; that is, only 'after that', in the dynamics of the process that develops, it (freely) passes from the *Es* to the *gibt*.

The *Ereignis*, as an event of appropriation, is Heidegger's attempt to think of this inevitably metaphysical passage in terms that are no longer onto-theological, but its exposition is obviously problematic as it constantly runs the risk of slipping between the forms of 'metaphysics' criticized by Heidegger himself. The juxtaposition with Schelling's Absolute and its theoretical outcomes allows us to see the *Ereignis* as the attempt to think of being from within, in its free becoming, and to therefore develop a form of 'positive philosophy'.

1

A new beginning for Western philosophy

The juxtaposition of Nietzsche's and Schelling's theories, in addition to being an interesting subject for historical-philological investigation aimed at establishing the former's possible knowledge of Schelling's philosophy, and thus quashing the belief that Nietzsche's opinion of the philosopher from Leonberg can simply be traced back to a generically negative assessment of German Idealism as a whole, is also and above all a theoretical axis around which it is possible to reconstruct an itinerary of thought that culminates in both the explosion of the *crisis* of the philosophical-rational project of Modernity and its possible overcoming.

In particular, I believe that a philological treatment aimed at showing how much of Schelling's thought Nietzsche may have encountered, and through which channels, together with the illustration of common readings that directed the two authors towards similar theoretical perspectives, can help to highlight reasons for a theoretical affinity, which explodes at the height of the *crisis* of modern rationalism, presenting itself, in my opinion, as a successful philosophical combination capable, among other things, of shaping the contemporary debate and suggesting possible ways out of the postmodern nihilistic drift.

The philosophical affinity between Schelling and Nietzsche as revealed in the twentieth century in particular by theorists such as Karl Jaspers, Martin

Heidegger and Karl Löwith is essentially summarized in the fact that, before the conceptual non-deducibility of the being, inasmuch as it simply *exists*, both philosophers identify the correspondence of the original being (inexhaustible and unprethinkable, not yet mediated by the intellect and indeed never completely *consummatum* within the concepts of reason) with the a-rational sphere of pure will: a sphere that exceeds (and precedes) rational unifications. Supposing *pure will* (without representation) as this origin and impossible grounding of being, Schelling and Nietzsche arrive – albeit along different paths – at a mutual *failure* that testifies to the fragility of the philosophical project of Modernity and the precariousness of its *false unifications*, made possible only by the claim that the *ratio* is an 'exclusive court' that judges the essential determination of being and that is able to solve within its concepts the totality of reality.

However, Schelling's and Nietzsche's critical phases do not culminate – as Heidegger would have it – in a sort of 'metaphysics of the will' that finally yields to irrationalism. In the ontological excess identified by the two philosophers and described (provisionally) as *pure will*, absolute Freedom breaks through as an inexhaustible source of being and as the 'impossible' grounding of a dynamic ontology, that is, of a form of 'ontology of freedom' which, going beyond the boundaries of onto-theology, recognizes in freedom itself (precisely because it is an inexhaustible source of being) its intimate essential affinity with the dynamic-real 'natural' ambit which, in a dialectical relationship with the Nothing of the Beginning, precedes any *form* of being.

1 History of an idea

In reconstructing the theoretical relationship between our authors, it is certainly not possible to resort to explicit quotations from Nietzsche: his references to Schelling are, in fact, relatively few and consist mostly in general evaluations of the Romantic era. However, believing that this meant that

Nietzsche did not know Schelling's work and that therefore it could not have influenced his philosophy, means coming to a rather hasty evaluation which does not take into account Nietzsche's cultural education nor the development of his method of philosophical production.

Although the theoretical affinity recorded between Schelling and Nietzsche takes on a certain theoretical depth, worthy of investigation, in authors such as Jaspers, Heidegger, Löwith, Schulz and (even if in a negative way) Lukács, who do not refer directly to a philological link between the two philosophers but merely underline the common aspects present in their respective *critical* phases of thinking, it is worthwhile in my opinion to verify the possible philological links since they probably conceal a privileged route to a hermeneutic understanding of the *relationship* and its possible results.

1.1 A historical-philological link

It is well known that Nietzsche knew at least in general terms the early Schelling, in particular *Ideas for a Philosophy of Nature* (1797) and *System of Transcendental Idealism* (1800). This can be deduced already from the notes that Nietzsche collected in 1868 for a dissertation that was 'partly philosophical and partly scientific on the concept of organic, starting with Kant' but which never saw the light of day and where Schelling's two titles appear in the references. However, it is also known that the affinity revealed by theorists such as Jaspers and Heidegger, through the attestation of a mutual failure which highlights the fragility and criticality of the philosophical-rational project of Modernity, presupposes some knowledge on the part of Nietzsche of the philosophy of Freedom and in particular of the results of Shelling's later philosophy (*Spätphilosophie*).

In addition, the work by Otto Kein, *Das Apollinische und das Dionysische bei Nietzsche und Schelling* (*The Apollonian and Dionysian in Nietzsche and Schelling*), published in Berlin in 1935, marks the beginning of studies on this suggestive philosophical bond, which takes into consideration

Schelling's reflections on mythology in his later speculations. In drawing a parallel with the mythological figures of Apollo and Dionysus within their respective philosophical paths, Kein does not, however, intend to establish a direct dependence on Schelling's figures of mythology within Nietzsche's approach, but rather to underline a continuity and a common 'romantic' mood (*Stimmung*) at the basis of their affinity. The reading of Herder's reflections on mythology, the knowledge and use of Creuzer's work (which certainly goes beyond romantic theses on the subject, and goes in the very direction preferred by both Schelling and Nietzsche) or of A.W. Schlegel's *Vorlesungen über schöne Literatur und Kunst* (*Lectures on Dramatic Art and Literature*), without forgetting the common interest in his brother Friedrich's work (who was, among other things, the first to use the contrast between Apollo and Dionysius), Schelling's philosophical friendship with Hölderlin and Nietzsche's veneration of the poet from Tübingen, are simply examples of a cultural affinity, which, however, do not fully explain the comparisons that have emerged over the years between two of the greatest contemporary philosophers.

It was Manfred Frank who stressed the incontrovertible affinity between Schelling and Nietzsche with regard to the figure of Dionysus. However, unlike Kein, in his books *Der kommende Gott* (*The Coming God*) (1982) and *Gott im Exil* (*God in Exile*) (1988) he did not limit himself to underlining the points in common, but rather he wanted to demonstrate the direct 'dependence' of Nietzsche's 'dionysology' on Schelling's definition of the philosophy of Mythology: a 'dependence' (*Abbängigkeit*) on the part of Nietzsche with respect to Schelling's interpretation that directly concerned the triadic figure of Dionysus and the doctrine of the Eleusinian Mysteries. The particular position of Zagreus, Bacchus and Iacchus (reunited to epitomize the doctrine of the Mysteries) and the general reference to the figure of Demeter, as the mother of Iacchus, just as they appear in paragraph 10 of *Geburt der Tragödie* (*The Birth of Tragedy*), leaves little room for doubt, according to Frank, about Nietzsche's direct knowledge of Schelling's 'dionysology'.

The passages that Frank emphasizes to highlight Nietzsche's use of Schelling's theses all belong to his *Spätphilosophie*, in clear contrast to the most widespread theory according to which Nietzsche knew, at most, some works by Schelling belonging to the early years but none of his subsequent philosophical developments. The idea apparent in Frank's work is that Nietzsche had learned about Schelling's theses on the myth of Dionysus first from Bachofen, his colleague in Basel and Schelling's pupil, and secondly from Burckhardt. It is, in fact, well known that Burckhardt attended Schelling's Berlin lectures in 1841-2 and therefore would have heard Schelling's mythological-Christological claims. It is difficult to imagine that Nietzsche never discussed with these illustrious colleagues a figure like Schelling and the latter's position on the myth of Dionysus, an issue that so impassioned Nietzsche, especially since while writing *Geburt* Nietzsche had borrowed Bachofen's *Gräbersymbolik* (*Tomb Symbolism*) several times and, thanks to Overbeck, had developed a friendship with Burckhardt.

The centrality of the figure of Dionysus in Nietzsche's philosophy is not, however, doubted when tracing points in common with the later Schelling, as this aspect is relatively marginal when not associated with the overall theoretical approach and therefore with the passage from negative philosophy to positive philosophy. The common reference to Dionysus must certainly be read as a mythical exemplification of the *crisis* of Modernity and of its possible overcoming, but above all it must be read in dialectical continuity with the doctrine of Christianity: if for Schelling Dionysus is a central figure within his positive philosophy, essentially representing the link in the transition from Mythology to Revelation, then for Nietzsche Dionysus is in contrast with the apostle Paul's reading of Christ and constitutes the tension towards the 'new beginning' represented by the *semper adveniens Übermensch*. Both unite the gods of Zagreus, Bacchus and Iacchus into a single deity, as stages of a theogonic process that will have a new beginning in the *adveniens* Dionysus, Iacchus. Both Schelling and Nietzsche insist on the figure of the third Dionysus as a precursor to the *future beginning*, represented in Schelling by Jesus and in

Nietzsche by the *Übermensch*, however, they do not fall within the 'modern' perspective where value is given by the *novum*, because the *new beginning* promised by Dionysus goes beyond the 'history of being', beyond any project of universal history.

Although already in *Philosophical Investigations into the Essence of Human Freedom* there are themes that decisively resurface in Nietzsche[1] and which anticipate the subsequent distinction between a negative philosophy and a positive philosophy, we know that in Nietzsche's official library there is no trace of any books by Schelling and that in the University of Basel's library records, where Nietzsche's interest in Dionysus essentially began, there is no mention of Nietzsche borrowing any of his works. Demonstration of direct influence is therefore rather complex.

It is worth noting, however, that by *Nietzsches Archiv*'s own admission, Max Oehlers' *Nietzsches Bibliothek* (Weimar, 1942), which aimed to list the texts present in Nietzsche's personal library, appears to be significantly incomplete. Even the most recent studies on Nietzsche's books[2] remain inevitably incomplete in this regard, and there is the possibility that Nietzsche may have seen some of Schelling's work, for example, at his friend Franz Overbeck's father-in-law's house, where, as can be seen from the correspondence, it seems that Nietzsche kept part of his library.[3]

Of course more than just a few clues suggest that Nietzsche may have indirectly known about Schelling's philosophy: think of the influence exerted by Emerson's essays, or of the secondary literature that in essence constitutes Nietzsche's knowledge of modern philosophy.[4] In addition to frequent references to Schopenhauer's works (known to be strongly influenced by Schelling's *Philosophical Investigations* with regards to the *Wollen* concept), Nietzsche's knowledge of Eduard von Hartmann's *Die Philosophie des Unbewussten* (*Philosophy of the Unconscious*) (Berlin, 1842) should not be forgotten – a text that from 1869 and into the 1880s was a constant source of reference for him during his definition of the Will to Power and the *doctrine of the eternal recurrence of the same*.[5] In that work von Hartmann believed that the Unconscious consisted of a fusion between Hegel's Idea and Schopenhauer's Will. As a union of Will and Reason, the Unconscious represented the absolute grounding of the existent, yet Will was in a prominent position with respect to Reason, and in this von Hartmann seemed to follow the theses of Schelling's positive philosophy. Moreover, in 1869, at the beginning of Nietzsche's period in Basel, von Hartmann published the essay '*Schellings positive Philosophie als Einheit von Hegel und Schopenhauer*' (*Schelling's positive philosophy as a unity of Hegel and Schopenhauer*) (Berlin, 1869). This short essay which, explicitly written on the basis of the *Sämtliche Werke* edited by Schelling's son and probably intended as a chapter in his *Philosophy of the Unconscious*, represents one of the first studies dedicated to Schelling's positive philosophy and interprets the philosophies of Schopenhauer and Hegel in the light of Schelling's positive philosophy, seeing Schopenhauer's Will as the real principle and Hegel's Idea as the ideal principle. Although it is not known whether Nietzsche read von Hartmann's texts on Schelling's positive philosophy directly, the attention he paid to *Philosophy of the Unconscious* does suggest a general interest in the author.

In 1996, with John Elbert Wilson's *Schelling und Nietzsche: zur Auslegung der frühen Werke Friedrich Nietzsches* (*Schelling and Nietzsche: On the Interpretation of Nietzsche's Early Works*), published for the *Monografien und Texte zur Nietzsche-Forschung* series, we see a real leap in quality within this attempt to verify the overlap between Schelling and Nietzsche even on a philological level. By his own admission, however, Wilson intended highlighting the Schellingian aspects within Nietzsche's work in order to contribute to the interpretation of his early philosophy during the *Geburt* phase. Overcoming Otto Kein's drawbacks, Wilson – author of, among other things, a work on Schelling's mythology[6] – develops Manfred Frank's hypotheses on the common reference to the myth of Dionysus, going beyond it and attempting to underline the Schellingian undercurrent to Nietzsche's work. The text looks at Nietzsche's philosophical conclusions and their possible 'proximity' to Schelling's work, with a reasoning that presents a plausible picture of Schelling's 'presence' (also and above all of his *Spätphilosophie*) in Nietzsche's works.

When considering Nietzsche's Will to Power and its sources, Schopenhauer's Will immediately comes to mind. This juxtaposition, however, even if philologically necessary in order to understand Nietzsche's thought at least until the mid-1870s, does not offer in itself an adequate penetration of the *Wille zur Macht* dynamics. If it is true that Nietzsche's 'Dionysian' is certainly initially traceable to the metaphysical concept of Will as it is described in Schopenhauer's *The World as Will and Representation*, representing the violation of the *principium individuationis* that limits Will within the bounds of representation, then it is even more true that for Nietzsche this does not constitute in any way the possibility for the negation of the Will in the *Noluntas*, but rather the necessary condition for the 'sanctification' of the original universal will in its general and chaotic character. For Schopenhauer the Will is extinguished in the non-will, while for Nietzsche the Will to Power turns towards ultra-empowering, towards the absolute intensification of the will as a universal 'principle'.[7]

The Apollonian-Dionysian 'dialectic' is useful to understand the development of the *Wille zur Macht* provided it is understood beyond the Schopenhauerian meaning of Will. The dynamic of the Will to Power is in fact articulated in three moments that recursively alternate: (1) initially the *Wille zur Macht* operates in the abyssal grounding of the 'Dionysian' as the will of the original being (in the *Urwesen* with which, according to Nietzsche during the *Geburt* years, 'we feel fused in the Dionysian ecstasy'); (2) then, as an individual principle, in the 'Apollonian' moment that determines the being in its possible and multiple forms and 'perspectives'; (3) finally, again in the Dionysian moment that demolishes the being and its forms in view of the overcoming. This last moment of the Will to Power is represented 'historically' by Nietzsche through the announcement of the 'death of God' and the infinite aspiration to the *Übermensch*.

1.2 A theoretical affinity

If on the historical-philosophical level Wilson's work probably represents the most important acquisition (although in my opinion there should be further investigation of, for example and as we shall see, the common effects that the reading of the *Kritik der Urteilskraft* (*Critique of Judgement*) and of Kant in general had on Schelling and Nietzsche, which for both were curiously mediated by contemporary readings of Plato's dialogues),[8] then on a more purely theoretical level we witness the emergence of a theoretical continuity with Schelling that is difficult to ignore in the great interpretations of Nietzsche's thought (Jaspers, Löwith and Heidegger) during the mid-1930s.

Thanks also to his deep knowledge of Schelling's thought,[9] Karl Jaspers was probably the first to underline, in his *Nietzsche, Einführung in das Verständnis seines Philosophierens* (*Nietzsche: An Introduction to the Understanding of His Philosophical Activity*) (Berlin, 1935), how Nietzsche's 'turn', after the 'death of God', basically replicated the same transition that Schelling made from negative philosophy to positive philosophy.

The contradiction into which, according to Jaspers, Nietzsche fell after *Tod Gottes* ('*mein Wort für „Ideale"*') (the death of God) between the elimination of every *Grund* and the need for a positive historical overcoming, and therefore of the position of new *Ideals*, suggests that Nietzsche followed in Schelling's footsteps[10] even without being familiar with them. Karl Jaspers joins Schelling's and Nietzsche's thought in a common destiny when they realize the insufficiency that the Ideal demonstrates before the Being inasmuch as it actually exists and whose existence is not rationally deducible.

Karl Löwith, too, starting with the interpretation of the theory of the eternal recurrence,[11] finds Schellingian echoes in Nietzsche that essentially build up around the supreme affirmation of the feature 'I am': in *Also sprach Zarathustra*, the final stage in the rapprochement to the figure of the *Übermensch* after the 'you must' and the 'I want', and the figure in which the will, no longer only human because it goes beyond a subject that possesses and uses it, finds itself again as a cosmic necessity[12] that can only coincide with absolute liberty.

Before moving on to Heidegger, who deserves special attention in this research context since it was most probably the juxtaposition he suggested that gave legitimate echo to other voices, it is necessary to dwell briefly on two other authors who in the 1950s both saw some affinity between Schelling and Nietzsche, even if from different positions; they are György Lukács and Walter Schulz.

Even if in a negative way, in his work *Die Zerstörung der Vernuft* (*The Destruction of Reason*) (Berlin, 1954), Lukács points out a possible juxtaposition between Schelling's work and Nietzsche's speculations, reading both of them as thinkers of 'irrationalism'. Starting with Schelling's concept of *intellectual intuition*, which represents the end of rationality and abandonment to the myths of fantasy, Lukács re-reads the history of contemporary German thought as the progressive distrust of reason that translates into the inability to consume reality in the thought and abandonment 'to the uncritical exaltation of intuition, to the aristocratic gnoseology, to the repudiation of historical-social progress, to the creation of *myths*'.[13] According to Lukács's interpretation, Nietzsche was the epigone of a story that began precisely with Schelling's irrationalism and that later translated on the practical-political level into the disaster of the Third Reich.

The work *Die Vollendung des deutschen Idealismus in der Spätphilosophie Schellings* (*The Completion of German Idealism in Schelling's Late Philosophy*) (Stuttgart, 1955) by Walter Schulz is of an altogether different kind, which instead of indicating in Hegel's thought the realization of the idealistic project and in Schelling's subsequent steps the fall into irrationalism, finds in Schelling's *Spätphilosophie* the continuation of the idealistic project brought to its completion-exhaustion.

If the principle of German Idealism is defined as the 'method of absolute reflection' and its underlying motive is 'the possibility of the self-constitution of pure subjectivity' (i.e. of the *Selbstvermittlung*, of self-mediation), then Schulz clarifies that by asking the question 'Why, in general, is there reason rather than non-reason?' the later Schelling does nothing but continue the idealistic discourse, taking it to its extreme consequences. In Schelling's late philosophy, the subjectivity that wants to take possession of itself experiences its own impotence for the first time, since the *fact* of its existence has always preceded its *thought*, and knowledge, coming up against its own limit, experiences this difference that is within itself: neither thought nor being, but pure indifference as their mediation.

Due to these developments, Schulz believes that Schelling should be read as part of the great post-idealist (or 'existentialist') thinkers among which he includes Nietzsche, whose work has a decisive place in the history of contemporary thought, coming in fact after Schelling and Kierkegaard.

As far as the theoretical side of the link between Schelling and Nietzsche is concerned, Heidegger's thinking is certainly central. The philosopher from Meßkirch who, as is well known, dealt with Nietzsche's work throughout his whole life in lectures, speeches and essays, had already in 1927–8, immediately after the publication of *Being and Time*, held a seminar in Marburg dedicated to Schelling's *Freiheitsschrift* (*Philosophical Investigations*), probably also inspired by the conversations he had with Karl Jaspers on the subject at the time. In Heidegger's seminar, whose notes have recently been published[14] together with the transcriptions of the participants who took turns in writing up the minutes, the themes of the most famous course that Heidegger held in 1936 in Freiburg are only hinted at.[15] In this latter course (*Vorlesung*), Heidegger established a clear theoretical affinity between Schelling and Nietzsche, precisely in the light of a common ontological concept that indissolubly and originally linked being and will, and that he would later confirm in his course on *Metaphysics of German Idealism* in 1941.

In addition to these lectures, Heidegger had the opportunity to stress in several places in his works the possibility of a certain 'link' between Schelling and Nietzsche starting from understanding being as will in the absolute sense – a thesis that would lead Schelling to the failure of his 'System' and therefore to literary silence, and Nietzsche to the inevitable overthrowing of metaphysics, as well as to the failure of his *Wille zur Macht* project.

Schelling's great merit was, according to Heidegger, that of having introduced will as the foundation of the speculative dialectic of idealism inasmuch as it coincides with the original being, thus 'quashing' the logical solution of the ontological nexus, or rather the claim that within the concept being and thought are fully and reciprocally converted. For this reason Schelling was, according to Heidegger, the thinker who 'pushes German idealism beyond its own fundamental position from within', and whose *Philosophical Investigations* 'shakes Hegel's *Logic* even before its appearance'.

2 From Heidegger to Schelling, via Nietzsche

In the theoretical path that I propose, we come to the idea that, starting from the juxtaposition between Nietzsche and Schelling, the Ontology of Freedom prefigured by Luigi Pareyson received a further thrust in the direction of an ontology that I define provisionally as *dynamic*, since the ontological priority assigned to freedom is superimposed on the dynamic-actual priority of the *Wirklichkeit* (reality as actuality), so as to determine precisely an original *dynamic* that, 'based' on the Nothingness of original freedom, actually commands (*drives*) an *ontology*. In this theoretical perspective, Heidegger's interpretation is certainly central.

If in Schelling the connection established between pure will and original freedom is evident in the transition from the philosophy of Identity to the philosophy of Freedom, where the freedom of the *Wesen* goes from 'executive' to 'constitutive', then in Nietzsche this theoretical overlap is not explicit in these terms yet is similarly reproduced in the dynamics of the Will to Power and in particular in the ontological excess that is described by the 'Dionysian' moment of the *Wille zur Macht*. Like the pure *Wollen* of Schelling's *Philosophical Investigations*, the Will to Power is not reduced, in fact, to the idealistic concept of will as a synthesis of *perceptio* and *appetitus*: the ontological excess described as pure will that resists being overlapped with knowledge coincides, in Schelling as in Nietzsche, with the post-metaphysical concept of ontological freedom: a concept that finds a very effective synthesis in the Heideggerian expression according to which it is not to be understood as the *Eigenschaft* (property as faculty) of the individual (whatever it is and however it is understood), because it is rather the individual (in its different expressions) that is the *Eigentum* (property in terms of possession) of freedom itself.

If in the first instance there is a juxtaposition between Schelling and Nietzsche – matured in the split highlighted by authors such as Jaspers, Löwith and Heidegger – which sees in the reasons for the failure that awaited both philosophers at the height of modern rationality the possibility of a *new beginning* for philosophy in the absolute Freedom of the non-grounding, then it is necessary to continue the path taken, investigating further the 'dynamics' of the eternal *Mögen* (Liking, or potency to will) and the *Wille zur Macht*, in particular connection with Nature as 'primordial living being': that original and primeval being, described in Schelling's *Weltalter* and analogously in Nietzsche's *Dionysian* vision of the world, which unites everything within itself and has nothing that precedes it, so that, as Löwith observes, 'as a consequence it must develop purely from itself, in the most spontaneous way and of its own will'.

This theme, used as a sign for the reconsideration of *Wille zur Macht* in its theoretical juxtaposition to the Will to Love of Schelling's *Philosophical Investigations into the Essence of Human Freedom*, was translated into the Heideggerian idea of a *Wider-Wille* (Contrary-Will) as activator and motor of the *Ursein* – found by Schelling in the *Liebe* and by Nietzsche in the complex dynamics of the Will to Power – within which I highlighted (also based on Emanuele Severino's acute theoretical observations on the originality of the *becoming* in Nietzsche's thought[16] as well as on the studies on *Wille zur Macht* conducted by Günther Abel and Wolfgang Müller-Lauter)[17] two 'moments' in tragic opposition and alternation: the *Dionysian* moment and the *Apollonian* moment.

The freedom of Schelling's eternal *Mögen* and the dynamics of Nietzsche's *Wille zur Macht* should be read in connection with the Openness of Nature, this latter a word in which 'the assonance of the primordial word φύσις still vibrates, which is also equated to the ζωή, which we translate as "life"

(*Leben*)', and 'the essence of life, which is thought of at the very beginning, is not presented in biological terms, but as φύσις, the Source'.[18] In this sense, the original dynamic that *commands* the transition to being and its forms can be neither Pure Will nor the Dionysian Will to Power, but first and foremost the absolutely free *command* of *love*, which opts inexorably for the existent, keeping it in its 'impossible grounding'. Aligning freedom with the *Physis* thus understood certainly leads to difficulties on the theoretical level, however the dynamic becoming that is introduced in this way has the undisputed merit of bringing the original freedom into the process, that is to say into the historical happening of being; this is in fact the merit of Nietzsche's insight that brings the original and permanent *Chaos des Alls* (Chaos of All) into the history of being.

In the space 'historically' opened by the 'death of God', an immediate *Chaos* erupts that bears every possible 'history of being' like a repressed memory: a non-grounding (*Un-grund*) devoid of reason, but infinitely charged with every *potency to be*, that emerges in moments of maximum *crisis* to regenerate every *new beginning*, in the form of an absolutely free *command* that essentially repeats the original dynamic of Schelling's *Liebe*.

In fact if, when considering the philosophies of Schelling and Nietzsche, it is easy to discover the main affinity by placing the Will in its purest expression at the origin of the All, then it is also true that the juxtaposition between the *Wille* and the *Ursein* (as *absolute Wirklichkeit*) derives essentially from the attempt to make 'humanly comprehensible', on the one hand, that indistinct *Chaos* from which come the possible determinations of being, and, on the other, the dynamic that decides them. After all, the Openness of Nature gives itself as *will* only and always in representation of a *knowledge* (*Wissen*) that in any case already deprives it of that original Freedom that distinguishes it; before the *will* lies in fact the free and absolute *command* of love, whose expression is pure and simple *Weisheit* (wisdom) in that it knows/is able 'to do', that is to say 'power, strength, dominion', 'because it is what is in everything, but, precisely for this reason, also what is above everything'.[19]

In the un-pre-thinkable of the *Wirklichkeit* (as *Chaos des Alls*, actuality as *chaos of All*) the Schellingian meaning of positive philosophy which describes it as *potentia potentiae* resonates; it sums up the unsolvable contrast between necessity and freedom that can only be 'solved' in Love (completely devoid of 'grounding') as its 'impossible Law'.

The Openness of Nature, which *after* the 'death of God' is discovered to be 'undeified and redeemed', is therefore proposed again in the *eternal Mögen* of the *Chaos des Alls* as the grounding of the grounding. In that Openness of *Chaos* present at the root of our soul, and at the grounding of Nature as a whole, there is in fact the possibility for the 're-betrothal' of man to the world, a 're-betrothal' that is, however, always a long way off (towards which we are 'turned' at most), and that never happens historically, because otherwise it would lose sight of its original and absolute Freedom.

In this sense we could accommodate the question posed by Massimo Cacciari, in continuity with his reading of the Overman, in the preface to *Vertigini della ragione*, that is whether one should understand the idea of the *Übermensch*, as an infinite tension to the overcoming, precisely as the maximum *command* to Dionysus to transform himself into *Nunc aeternum, Aión*. Precisely in the 'last seal' of Nietzsche's love, that is, in the acceptance of the *eternal recurrence of the same*, the moment is, in fact, returned to its abyssality, that is to say to the becoming of *Chaos* considered *aionically* and therefore beyond any distinction decided in Time.

The connection of freedom with the Openness of Nature and with Love's command can certainly account for the dynamics of the *Wille zur Macht*, but it does not fully restore the ontological concept of Schelling's freedom that lives its essential dialectical conflict with the Nothingness of the beginning. On this course, Heidegger plays a fundamental role in particular with the *Nichts* of the *Was ist Metaphysik?* conference in 1929, which Pareyson (and Walter Schulz before him, though for different reasons) believed should be read in conjunction with the Freedom in Schelling's *Philosophical Investigations*.

2.1 System and freedom

Placing the a-rational of Will at the beginning, Schelling and Nietzsche arrive at a double failure, represented on the one hand by Schelling's inability to conclude the discourse undertaken in his *Philosophical Investigations*, where, by further investigating the theme of Will, he finally comes to illuminate the absolute freedom of the original; and represented, on the other hand, by Nietzsche's failure in the realization of his most complete *theoretical* work, *Der Wille zur Macht*, coinciding with the empowering of the idealistic Will.

> If Schelling did not present a completed published work, this was due to the type of problem that he had been working on since the treatise on *freedom*.
> Nietzsche, 'the only essential thinker after Schelling', also failed in his main work, *Will to Power*, and for the same reasons. But this dramatic double failure of the great thinkers is not actually a failure and should not be considered negatively: quite the contrary. It is the rise of that which is totally other, the spark of a new beginning. Anyone who truly knows the reason for this failure and, knowing it, overcomes it, should become the founder of a new beginning in Western philosophy.[20]

To clarify the meaning of this quotation by Heidegger, which dates back to the 1936 *Vorlesung*, we must first reflect on the reasons for these failures in order to understand in particular (1) what difficulties both Schelling and Nietzsche came up against in the most acute and critical phases of their respective speculative paths, in order to then identify (2) what goals Schelling and Nietzsche actually intended to achieve according to Heidegger. And, finally, we must try to understand (3) what Heidegger actually meant by the expression *new beginning* for Western philosophy.

The suggestion that the passage in question inevitably gives rise to also invites us to proceed with a certain amount of caution: in short, we must resist the temptation to take Heidegger's words too seriously. At the same time, however, we cannot avoid considering Heidegger's 'prophecy' also in the light of postmodern philosophical outcomes. The questions that accompany the analysis of this passage can in fact be condensed essentially into a single issue that guides the introductory part of Schelling's *Philosophical Investigations*, to which Heidegger devoted special attention in his 1936 course: that is, the question of the possibility of a 'System' of knowledge in a philosophy that places the abyss of ontological Freedom at the 'centre'. Without having to investigate the ramifications within which this issue is articulated, we can immediately affirm that in the 1936 *Vorlesung* Heidegger considered Schelling and Nietzsche the two thinkers against whom the *philosophical project of Modernity* irreparably foundered, meaning by that expression the continuous philosophical tension directed at the *rational-systematic* constitution of knowledge, which finds its highest expression in the theses of Hegelian Idealism.

The two great failures of modern philosophy can be read as the effect of the *crisis* of the *philosophy of unconditional reason* itself (and of the conceptual system that derives from it), which claims to resolve the totality of being within its own concepts and to deduce the All starting from its own principle. In such a theoretical context, it is certainly necessary to understand the expression *crisis* in its dynamic meaning as splitting/separation. The distinction itself between a positive philosophy and a negative philosophy is to be interpreted as the inevitable development of a *crisis*, that is to say of an essential and radical conflict and schism (*Auseinandersetzung, Scheidung*): a separation that follows and accompanies the ontological distinction between the *Wirklichkeit* (actuality) and the *Denken* (thinking). At the same time, it is therefore necessary to think of the expression *crisis* in its *dynamic-temporal* meaning, since it indicates a development, a process, which takes place in time, by reason of the forces and powers coessential to the original being, which determine in their effectiveness (*Wirksamkeit*) the conceptual sphere, as well as its inevitable *saturation* before the original unprethinkable being.

In Schelling as in Nietzsche, philosophical reflection is not simply the application of a theoretical apparatus to the reality of what exists: it is rather coessential to the existent itself. Schelling's same distinction between *negative* (or rational) philosophy and *positive* philosophy is not the mere rendering of reason before the being insomuch as it simply exists, nor is it the arbitrary separation of fields of knowledge; rather, it springs from an original and conflicting need (never definitively reconcilable conceptually) within the existent itself. In fact, Heidegger himself observed, in illustrating the theoretical path of *Philosophical Investigations* which aims to ensure the possibility of a System that places Freedom at the centre, that 'Schelling thinks of forces in positions of will, he thinks of the conflict of wills that do not allow themselves to be reconciled by means of a conceptual artifice'.[21]

The same applies to the *pars destruens* and *pars construens* of Nietzsche's philosophy, which are not to be read as deriving from an intellectual interpretation arbitrarily applied to the existent from the outside, but as the necessary 'manifestation' of the existent itself, insomuch as the latter is always and only a Will to Power, meaning an area of absolute and conflictual *Wirklichkeit*, whose dynamics and actuality can never be understood conceptually once and for all.

For both Schelling and Nietzsche, what counts in the end is the expression according to which the *crisis* of their respective philosophies can be defined as the 'dynamic development' of their problematic *unity*, through which the conflict between two mutually opposed internal tensions is founded at the same time: one tending to the conservation and strengthening of the 'form' achieved, the other aimed at overcoming and emancipating any will to persist *in* the form. All according to a continuous oscillation that is encapsulated by Nietzsche in the conceptually irreconcilable dialectic between the *Apollonian* and the *Dionysian*.

This common splitting or *crisis* that (certainly in continuity with Karl Löwith and Karl Jaspers) I detect in the crucial moments of the philosophies of Schelling and Nietzsche depends, in my opinion, (1) on a certain concept of 'being' that our authors develop, (2) on a coessential and *original will* that both philosophers place at the very heart of being and, finally, (3) on a consequent *organic theory of time*, which for both takes a rotatory form (for

Schelling through the various attempts at *Weltalter*, for Nietzsche through the controversial doctrine of the *eternal recurrence of the same*), in order to capture in an overall 'System of knowledge' this *dynamic* concept of being inasmuch as it is 'time' and therefore eternal becoming.

Although more than once Nietzsche pointed out that he believed the 'will to system' should be understood as a 'disease of character'[22] or as 'a form of immorality [...] for a thinker,'[23] it is in any case known that in his Will to Power project he attempted to assign a renewed and organic form of System to his philosophy and related concepts.

Already in 1872, Nietzsche thought of the possibility of a systematic form of knowledge *as* art,[24] and later in the third book of *The Gay Science* he described the 'organic system' as the unity of art, knowledge and practical wisdom of life, a goal philosophy should aim for.

> And we are still a long way off from the time when artistic forces and *practical wisdom of life* will unite with scientific thought; a long way off from the formation of a higher *organic system* in relation to which the erudite, the doctor, the artist and the legislator, as we know them today, would look like wretched relics.[25]

In this 'new' definition of System one immediately notices the role that the concept of *life* (*Leben*) assumes: a concept that was of particular importance to Nietzsche as early as 1868 when, in considering Kant's teleology in the *Critique of Judgement*, and with an idea that was later abandoned to write a partly philosophical and partly scientific dissertation on teleology *after Kant*, he thought of the distinction (probably of materialistic derivation) between *life* (*Leben*) and *forms* (*Formen*), which the intellect can grasp from that life.

The concept of *life* anticipates and lays the foundation for the subsequent concept of the Will to Power, within which Nietzsche tried to resolve both the intellect (which can no longer be understood as something external to the *life* that it knows how to grasp the *forms* from, but as the expression of *life* itself that emerges on the surface) and the forms of the *living* (*das Lebendige*; but we could also speak of the original living, or *Urlebendiges*, as expressed by Schelling in the language of the *Weltalter-Phase*), in a dynamic becoming that returns eternally to itself and that is already described by the same recursiveness that is present in the expression 'will to power', in the sense described by Karl Löwith.

As is well known, in the definition of an 'organic system' the concept of *life* is of great significance for Schelling too and this, among other things, depends in all probability on the common and intense reading of the teleological section of Kant's *Kritik der Urteilskraft* (*Critique of Judgement*), in which the definition of 'organism' – described as what is *cause and effect of itself* (*von sich selbst*) – clearly emerges, and the consequent perception of an Absolute as *Gesamtorganismus* (total organism).

If it is possible to sustain that Schelling's philosophy orbits around one single great thought, this can certainly be represented by the attempt to turn knowledge about the totality of being into a System. In fact, from his first writings the objective was to identify a principle (*Grund-satz*) from which to deduce all the individual and possible propositions (*Sätze*). If this constitutes a plausible definition of the System when it is of a purely conceptual (i.e. formal) nature, then certainly the discourse changes when one assumes – as Schelling himself does, attributing an ontological priority to Nature over Spirit in the development of his philosophy – the *existent*, as an (elusive and dynamic) sphere that always precedes the *concept*, as the object of knowledge. Precisely by virtue of this ontological priority assigned to Nature (as a self-placing), the particular *temporal-dynamic* interpretation of being determines a form of 'System' that certainly goes beyond the conceptual definition mentioned above, and must assume the original Freedom as the absolute *effectuality-actuality* of being itself at the 'centre', as the (conceptually) impossible grounding.[26]

Such a concept of original freedom was forced to come to terms with the Nothing of the Beginning, and on this path one cannot but highlight the radicality of Schelling's position with respect to that of Nietzsche: a radicality that emerges in all its theoretical effectiveness precisely in consideration of Heidegger's interpretation.

The critical juxtaposition between Schelling and Nietzsche, proposed by Heidegger in the 1936 *Vorlesung*, basically leads towards a thought of absolute (ontological) freedom, as the foundation of being and entity, and in this sense the Heideggerian *Ereignis* is well placed, on the one hand, to summarize the indissoluble (coessential) link with time and, on the other, to obviate a concept that thinks of being as still and only beginning with the existent.

In fact, the concurrence of Will and Being, which Heidegger insists on in placing Schelling alongside Nietzsche, is not able to present freedom in its ontological character.

The expression '*Wollen ist Ursein*' in Schelling's *Philosophical Investigations* can be misleading: such a conceptual overlap is not, in fact, to be read – as Heidegger would like – in the sense of a 'metaphysics of the will', since this would mean assuming a 'will' that, subordinate to reason, ends up coinciding with it entirely, restoring in addition a deducible metaphysical principle starting from being as existent.

On the contrary, Schelling's perspective (like Nietzsche's) offers a completely different concept of the 'will', which, on the one hand, certainly not only translates into the rational form that thinks of being as existent (and in this responds perfectly also to the philosophical project of Idealism) but, on the other hand, also stands as an *excess* that is never completely consumable, as a resource of the same rational form and finally as a free and permanent (absolute) Principle of Being.

The possibility of understanding being as *Ereignis* is already mentioned in Schelling's and Nietzsche's 'critical' conclusions, and this can be essentially based on a concept of the will that exceeds the idealistic pretensions of saturating Reality in the theory about Reality itself.

In Schelling as in Nietzsche, in fact, will is never completely reduced to reason and forms of thought, nor can one speak of a will that essentially coincides with the 'will' of 'unconditioned representing'.

> Everything in the world, as we see it now, is rule, order and form: but nevertheless in the background there is always the irregular, as if all of a

sudden it could reappear, and nowhere is that order and that form found in the original condition, but everywhere things appear as if a condition originally devoid of rule has been brought towards order.

This is the elusive basis of reality in things, the excess that never disappears, that which, no matter how much effort is made, is never resolved in the intellect, but always remains in the grounding.[27]

This irreducible *excess*, as an *un-pre-thinkable non-grounding* (*Un-grund*) of being, is not to be understood exclusively as a fixed and motionless excess, but – as we will see – as a 'dynamic' sphere in a dialectical relationship with Heidegger's *Nichts* from the *Was ist Metaphysik?* lecture.

From this point of view, *being as an event* appears in its unavoidable bond with time, not as if the event were a manner of being, nor, vice versa, as if being were a manner of the event, but only in the sense that the event is what 'makes happen' and destines the being (allowing it to be present), and what ultimately offers time.

Insofar as being is event, the event is 'what makes happen', only this can be said of the event and of its inexhaustible origin without falling into the thinking that starts from a grounding: *Ereignis ereignet*.

What is intended is that metaphysics, in the Heideggerian meaning of the 'history of being' that thinks and structures being starting from the consideration of the entity, certainly reaches its fulfilment in Nietzsche's nihilism, but this destiny that allows one to understand being, beyond the grounding, in fact as *Ereignis*, already appears in the a-rational *excess* that Schelling proposes as ontological freedom, that is to say as an impossible grounding (*Un-grund*) of being.

And this Freedom can only be indissolubly linked to Nothingness, because only in this higher-relationship does the (ontological) dynamic that follows from it exist.

Heidegger's *Ereignis* in some ways repeats the dynamics of the *Wille zur Macht* and in particular Schelling's freedom in its higher-relationship to

Nothingness, since it is intended as a *make happen*: a destinating (*Schicken*) of the being, from which, however, *Who* destines as much as the destinating itself 'abstain' (in fact, in the *Nichts*).

> In order to think about being itself [...] one has to look away from it, if by 'being' one means – as happens in all metaphysics – what is explored and interpreted exclusively starting from the entity and in view of the entity, understood as its grounding.
>
> To think 'Being' explicitly requires us to relinquish Being as the ground of beings in favour of the giving which prevails concealed in unconcealment, that is in favour of the *Es of es gibt*, namely the 'it' that gives.[28]

2
Heidegger's reading of Schelling

1 *Essentia et existentia*

The origin of the so-called fracture of being, which determines Schelling's and Nietzsche's double failure, and in particular the division in Schelling between a negative and a positive philosophy, lies, as is known, in a question that is central to all German Idealism, namely the problem of *Wirklichkeit*, of 'actuality'. Specifically, it is the particular concept of actuality proposed by Hegel that constitutes the problem against which Schelling's philosophy critically fights and develops, starting with his *Philosophical Investigations* from 1809.

Schelling was not the only one to criticize Hegel's concept of actuality; on the contrary, it can be argued, using Löwith,[1] that precisely in the reflection on this concept and on Hegel's separation of 'logical' conciliation between reason and actuality, the conditions for overcoming the latter's philosophy matured in thinkers such as Ruge, Feuerbach, Marx and Kierkegaard, as well as in Russian thinkers who widely confronted the theses of German Idealism, paying particular attention to Schelling's reflections.

Ruge preferred to address the *ethical-political* existence of the *community*, Feuerbach the sensitive existence of the physical man, Marx the economic existence of the masses, and Kierkegaard the ethical-religious existence of the individual. In Ruge, historical existence is revealed in political 'interest', in Feuerbach real existence is generally found in sensation and passion, in Marx social existence is revealed in sensitive activity as a social practice, and in Kierkegaard ethical reality is shown in the practice of intimate action.[2]

Such critiques, arising from the different readings of the concept of *Wirklichkeit*, determine, each for itself, the different outcomes in line with the peculiarities and intentions of the thinkers who elaborate them. In particular, for Marx and Kierkegaard, the Hegelian assumption that 'what is rational is real and what is real is rational' determines a philosophy that conforms to reality, but only what concerns the 'understanding' of reality itself, and this clashes with the Marxist idea (inasmuch as it is linked to a political practice) and the Kierkegaardian idea (inasmuch as it is linked to the existential and religious condition of man in the world) of a philosophy that *must be realized* – which, in short, must be able to be implemented in the life of man, as an individual immersed in society. In any case, it is a criticism that remains anchored to the existential dimension of *being-there (Dasein)*.

Looking closely, the most radical criticism of Hegel's *Wirklichkeit* capable of shifting the discourse onto an ontological level, and not a practical-social one, nor an existential (and religious) or banally ontic one, is Schelling's criticism and the consequent division of positive philosophy from negative philosophy: in fact, only Schelling's critical reading allows us to deepen reflection on Hegel's *Wirklichkeit* in the perspective of an *ontological realism*.

In his fundamental *From Hegel to Nietzsche: The Revolution in Nineteenth-Century Thought*, Karl Löwith underlines how Schelling, in separating the *existentia* and the *essentia* held together by Hegel, makes substantial use of the pre-critical Kant. On the basis of the distinction between *existentia* and *essentia* – which comes under the umbrella of the philosophy of scholasticism and according to which every created being is distinguished except God (in whom *essentia* and *existentia* are united) – the so-called ontological argument as a conceptual tool for demonstrating the existence of

God, among other things, could arise. This argument was, as is well known, the object of Kantian refutation as early as the 1763 essay *The Only Possible Argument in Support of a Demonstration of the Existence of God*: a refutation that was based substantially on a doctrine of being that distinguished being as *absolute position* (*absolute Setzung*) from the *relative being of predication*. Such a distinction is at the basis of the ontology of Schelling's *Spätphilosophie*, as well as – as we shall see – of the predicative-transitive concept of being that follows it. However, the *existentia* at the basis of Schelling's philosophy does not have the character of a steadfast grounding at all, rather, it becomes clear – on the basis of a radical rethinking of the relationship between Being and Time – as a free dynamic that escapes onto-theological considerations and that we find in the ontological concept of Heidegger's second phase and in particular in the notion of *Ereignis*.

According to Löwith, taking up Kant's thesis, the split highlighted by Schelling between *essentia* and *existentia* in fact constitutes the theoretical premise for Martin Heidegger's subsequent analyses, in particular for the existential analytics of *Sein und Zeit*.

> In the movement that was a reaction to Hegel, the problem of being already came to the point, with Schelling, where it would be taken up later by Heidegger. Who could deny that the 'actuality' of existence – inherent in the *factum brutum* of the 'that-is' – i.e. Heidegger's 'being thrown into the world' and 'projecting oneself into the future' do not correspond to Schelling's 'real existent' and to the 'ripping itself' from this necessary fortuitousness?[3]

Löwith is clear in presenting the issue: on the basis of a theoretical awareness acquired in the passage from the philosophy of Identity to the philosophy of Freedom, Schelling opposes the *existentia* of positive philosophy to the Hegelian *Wirklichkeit* totally resolved in the Concept. Although the position reached by Schelling in his *Philosophical Investigations* seems to be a solution to the existential problem of human freedom, on closer reflection, the problem of freedom in Schelling is first of all of an ontological-metaphysical nature and this marks a – if nothing else initial – distance from the Heidegger of *Being and Time* that remains anchored to an existential-style concept:

> Differently to Schelling, however, Heidegger builds a 'system of being-there' upon Kierkegaard's foundations, which completely lacks Schelling's tension between the negative philosophy of 'reason' and the positive philosophy of 'existence'. For him the general 'essence' of being-there is only and precisely in the particular 'existence' of each one who is unaware of where he comes 'from' and 'where' he is headed, who simply has the task of 'being', while assuming as 'guilt' the innocence of existing, that is, the not-being-responsible. The Hegelian 'being', which for Schelling was a simple 'potency to be' in the sense of possibility, while remaining opposed to reality, becomes for Heidegger an ontological determination belonging to 'real existence'.[4]

What Löwith claims is that, at the height of his negative philosophy, Schelling had already reached the point from which Heidegger could later begin his own existential analytics. Although it is not directly explained, the philosophical premise from which Heidegger takes his cue is constituted by the 'abyss' opened by Kant and illustrated clearly by the *madman* from Nietzsche's *Gay Science* with the announcement of the 'death of God'. The theoretical premise upon which – with Heidegger – the 'foundation' for twentieth-century existentialism is laid, which in some ways seems to translate into a passage from metaphysics to anthropology, is that same 'abyss of reason' which opens with the exhaustion of the Kantian transcendental Ideal. As soon as we read the apex of Schelling's negative philosophy in close connection with the exhaustion of the capacity of the idea of totality before the necessary existence of God, but more generally before the Existent as becoming, we understand how the possible overcoming (and therefore the passage to the 'positive') must be understood as a philosophy capable of being based on the *abyssal* Freedom of that existence (which is basically *grundlos*, without grounding).

> The merely existent is pure idea, yet it is not idea in the sense that the word has in negative philosophy. The merely existent, instead, is the being in which every (negative) idea, that is, every power, is excluded. We can therefore only call it the *inverted* idea (*die umgekehrte Idee*), the idea in which reason is placed *outside of itself*.
>
> Reason can place the existent, in which it is not yet anything of a concept, of a 'what', only as an absolute *outside of itself* [...]: reason is therefore, in this placing, placed outside of itself, absolutely ecstatic.[5]

In (placing-)grasping the merely existent (*das bloß Seyende*), reason is placed outside of itself because negative philosophy is only able to enlighten the possibility of that necessarily existent being, and certainly not to conclusively attest to its existence. However, this possibility of the existent has the nature of an unconditional necessity, since it constitutes our absolute need *des Trägers aller Dinge*, of the support of all things. Even if we are dealing with the unconditional need to place the existent, rationally this need does not prove anything.

According to Schelling, Kant penetrated into the absolute necessity of reason to admit an Existent without grounding and has established its *a priori* incomprehensibility. As long as reason becomes an object to itself, it finds as immediate content only the infinite potency to be; however, when it places itself outside itself, it knows how to grasp the space opened to the infinitely Existent: 'an immediate concept of reason, to which reason free of itself, inasmuch as it is not an object of itself – that is, immediate reason –, does not need to arrive at through reasoning, which is moreover so natural and inevitable'.[6]

Here we are at the pinnacle of negative philosophy and the beginning of positive philosophy. At the top of rational thought, one inevitably arrives at the thought of a necessarily Existent, without any grounding, a God free from rational demonstrations, whose existence can rationally only be hypothesized. On the other hand, Nietzsche, faced with the exhaustion of being understood as grounding, finds the Existent in the form of the All-becoming. Nietzsche's

God who dies represents the ontological construction *par excellence*, the ultimate grounding, the Supreme Good, the ultimate cause, what allows entities to become *phenomenologically*, that is, 'apparently' to pass from nothing to being to then return to nothing; but beyond his death opens a space, forbidden to reason, which illuminates the possibility of the Existent that is necessary in the sense that it is free and absolutely (ontologically, not *phenomenologically*) *becoming*.

The horizon opened by the 'death of God' is constituted by the fracture between the essence (*Wesen*) inasmuch as it exists, and the essence inasmuch as it is simply the grounding of existence: the ontological opening into which we are *thrown* consists in the rupture of the *Seinsfuge*, of the *juncture* of being, that is, of that point of union between grounding and existence which is thematized by Schelling in his 1809 *Philosophical Investigations into the Essence of Human Freedom*, but the question cannot be taken up and resolved simply on the existential level of the *Dasein*; on the contrary, it must be elevated and accepted on the ontological plane as Schelling does and as Heidegger will in some ways try to do after the 'turn' (*Kehre*).[7]

If we think of the expectations that arose in Berlin among the old and new Hegelians while waiting for the lectures on Schelling and at the same time reflect on the disappointment that many of them felt with the development of that philosophical 'discourse', we probably have the key to understanding a fundamental juncture of contemporary philosophy.

As has been widely noted (by authors such as Fuhrmann, Habermas, Löwith and Frank), with respect to Hegel's panlogistic system, Schelling was more or less unanimously credited with having highlighted, as his greatest objection, the *Wirklichkeit* as absolutely unsolvable in the Concept. On the other hand, the disappointment felt by many – Kierkegaard first and foremost – lay mostly in the discourse that Schelling could develop in his positive philosophy precisely from such an acquisition: a discourse that, in fact, could not be translated into the impulse to act historically defined or into a sort of analytic of human existence. From this point of view, one can understand what role Marx's and Kierkegaard's philosophies played (among the various objections to Schelling's developments of the concept of absolute *Wirklichkeit*) in the advancement of philosophical thought after the negative 'culmination' represented by the rational conclusions of the later Schelling.

In the historical-critical reconstruction conducted by Löwith in his *From Hegel to Nietzsche*, Heidegger would only resume the discourse from the point where Schelling had interrupted it, so to speak. However, if Heidegger can proceed with the existential analysis of *Sein und Zeit*, even starting with the Kierkegaardian approach which privileges the existence of man over a concept of *Wirklichkeit* that, in his view, remains an empty claim, it is probably Nietzsche's 'positive' philosophy that more faithfully (though unconsciously) follows the path opened by the Schelling of positive philosophy. With his attempt to philosophize starting with the historical and theoretical assumption of the 'death of God', Nietzsche traces more faithfully and coherently Schelling's intent beyond a merely existentialistic reading, and with the tension to the Overman understood well beyond a simple Feuerbachian anthropological inversion, moves (and brings back) Schelling's question onto purely ontological ground. Moreover, as has rightly been observed,[8] the positive Nietzsche of the aspiration to overcoming, that overcoming which according to Heidegger, however, Nietzsche would not accomplish because he was still restricted by the *Wille zur Macht* understood as a metaphysical principle, undoubtedly plays a fundamental role in Heidegger's ontological turn, that is, clarification of the problem and of its solution from the *Dasein* to the being itself.

In fact, the 'death of God' certainly also sanctions the death of the Subject, but this goes far beyond the simple evasion of the conflicts in metaphysics and in particular in German Idealism: the 'death of God' and the consequent tension to the unrepresentable figure of the *Übermensch* introduce an overcoming of any form of humanism in the recovery of an original Φύσις (*Physis*), which constitutes from within every form of being, including the so-called essence of man. It is a recovery of 'nature' as a free grounding that is undoubtedly the basis of Schelling's own entire theoretical path.

On the other hand, the Nietzschean concept of the *Übermensch* embodies the *naturalization* of man. The post-metaphysical man, aware of the 'death of God', recognizes himself as Nature, and rediscovers in himself that same *Chaos des Alls* that animates Nature as a whole. But such a discovery is only a first step; in order for the *naturalization* of man to be said to be accomplished in the transvaluation of every value, it is necessary that a 'new' *humanization* of Nature is also realized: which is the assignment of a new meaning to the earth as a continuous aspiration to the *Übermensch*.

The existentialist conclusions in the 1927 *Sein und Zeit*, which according to Löwith seem to start on the basis of the theses of Schelling's positive philosophy on being as existent, will find with the *Kehre* ('turn') a different and certainly more coherent orientation than the ontological concept that is at the basis of both Schelling's and Nietzsche's 'positive philosophy'. In order to understand the sense of being, Heidegger no longer turns to the *Dasein* but to the being itself and its historical dynamics, that is, to the 'history of being'. It cannot be excluded that this 'turn' and its 'theoretical content' were also influenced by the readings of the works of Schelling and Nietzsche, which Heidegger was able to conduct in greater depth after 1927. It is known, for example from the correspondence with Karl Jaspers, that in the composition of *Sein und Zeit* – accelerated by the author for academic reasons and which remained, as is known, unfinished – Heidegger's knowledge of Schelling's works was rather approximate; however, it is also known that already in the academic year 1927/8 he wanted to devote a seminar entirely to *Philosophical Investigations into the Essence of Human Freedom*. It is interesting to try to understand how much of the subsequent 'turn' is already in seed form in *Sein und Zeit* and in particular in the reasons for its incompleteness, and whether the contents of this 'turn' do not in fact have their roots in that third part of *Being and Time* that in

Heidegger's plans should have had as its title the reversal of the main title of his masterpiece: *Time and Being*.

In § 8 of *Sein und Zeit*, Heidegger writes what he intended the overall plan of the work to be:

Part One: The Interpretation of *Dasein* in terms of temporality, and the explication of time as the transcendental horizon for the question of Being.

Part Two: Basic features of a phenomenological destruction of the history of ontology, with the problematic of Temporality as our clue. Part One has three divisions:

1. The preparatory fundamental analysis of *Dasein*;
2. *Dasein* and temporality;
3. Time and Being.

Part Two likewise has three divisions:

1. Kant's doctrine of schematism and time, as a preliminary stage in a problematic of Temporality;
2. The ontological foundation of Descartes' '*cogito sum*', and how the medieval ontology has been taken over into the problematic of the '*res cogitans*';
3. Aristotle's essay on time, as providing a way of discriminating the phenomenal basis and the limits of ancient ontology.[9]

In 1926, finding himself needing to publish in order to see his appointment in Marburg as successor to Nicolai Hartmann confirmed, and not having completed the project of *Sein und Zeit* in its entirety, Heidegger decided to send only the First Part to the Ministry, though leaving out the third section 'Time and Being', and promising to publish what was missing in the work in a second volume, which however never saw the light of day, at least under that title. From the reconstruction of Heidegger's complete works, it seems that the material for the first section of Part Two corresponds to the book *Kant and the Problem of Metaphysics* published in 1929 and then as Volume III of the *Gesamtausgabe*. Regarding the third section of the First Part, which should have been entitled 'Time and Being', we know that Heidegger anticipated a first draft between April 1926 and May 1927, but that this – as was only made known in 1977 by the editor of the *Gesamtausgabe* edition of *Sein und Zeit* – was destroyed immediately after its drafting. Also in May 1927, Heidegger elaborated a second version of 'Time and Being' which corresponded to the text of the lectures of the summer semester, which – at the behest of Heidegger himself – was published in 1975 as the first edition of the *Gesamtausgabe* (with the title *Die Grundprobleme der Phänomenologie* [*Fundamental Questions of Phenomenology*] in the volume GA 24) and presented, as a note states, as a 'new elaboration of the third section of the First Part of *Being and Time*'.

When, several years later, Heidegger decided to name one of his conferences in 1962 *Time and Being*, his path of thought had so 'turned' with respect to the themes of existential analytics that it would certainly be wrong to think of that text as yet another version of the third section of Part One of *Sein und Zeit*; and yet, by assigning that evocative title, Heidegger certainly intended to reconnect with the central theme of *Sein und Zeit*, albeit at that time from a completely different perspective: to look, that is, at the thing itself, that is to say at being, in its difference from the entity and in its essential relationship to time, in the conviction that that was where the central point of the reflection on being was.

We will see how the contents of that conference are crucial to understand the evolution of Heidegger's thought in terms of 'positive philosophy' and in relation to comparisons with Schelling and Nietzsche.

It is certainly not intended to be argued that *Sein und Zeit* would have found a definitive and complete form if, at the time, Heidegger had taken Schelling's work dedicated to freedom directly into consideration or if, in drawing up his masterpiece, he had dealt directly with Nietzsche's *Wille zur Macht* and with the thought of the *eternal recurrence of the same*. What I want to emphasize instead is that already in the second half of the twenties, and then in the following decade, Schelling's and Nietzsche's theoretical impetus and their respective failures represent in the eyes of Heidegger that *Waldlichtung* – I adopt this misuse of Heidegger's terminology – in the middle of the dense knitting of the wood on the metaphysical horizon: that rift opened on the Being, or rather that irruption of the original being in the history of metaphysics, capable of illuminating (*lichten*) an Open space (precisely!) fundamentally veiled and forgotten by the metaphysical forest (*Wald*) of Western thought.

When considering the Hegelian concept of *Wirklichkeit*, the new and old critics of Hegel's system constantly laid their hopes on the possible recovery of true reality, which they understood to have been betrayed even by the later Schelling when, after the failure of the *Weltalters* attempts, he made that concept (already enlightened in some ways through the juncture of being [*Seynsfuge*] unveiled in the *Philosophical Investigations*) the premise for a 'positive' (historical to be precise) discourse aimed at the metalogical *narratives* of the Mythology and Revelation phases. The developments that – to recall only the most significant – on the one hand, Marx (via Feuerbach) and, on the other, Kierkegaard produced, starting from a new concept of *Wirklichkeit*, which mainly focused on the being-there of man, abandoning (or at least eluding) the *historical-ontological* space that the fracture of being had produced and that required investigation and study on that level.

In Nietzsche, we find the attempt to fill that gap; it is through his thought, in fact, that we can shed light on the fact that the opening of being, which is the fundamental aspect of the *ek-sistere*, is precisely the revelation of the abyssal grounding of the non-grounding, of the *Un-grund*, which as original being is pure and simple *Wollen*: a will that opens to being not as some existential determination, nor historically defined, but as the permanent Beginning (*das Bleibende*), as absolute, chaotic and free Compossibility of the origin: that *potentia potentiae* that is, finally, the *Wirklichkeit* mentioned by the later Schelling. If this theoretical affinity is not grasped, one inevitably ends up relegating the philosophies of Schelling and Nietzsche to a purposeless irrationalism. Vice versa, if we appreciate this theoretical continuity, we are able to grasp the meaning of the Heideggerian 'turn' in the sense of a form of 'positive philosophy' made possible by that 'fracture of being' highlighted by Schelling's and Nietzsche's 'crises'.

Returning to Löwith's reference to the theoretical closeness between Heidegger's existential analytics and the passage established between Schelling's negative and positive philosophy, in § 29 of *Sein und Zeit* we read that the factuality of existence inherent in the *factum brutum* of 'that is' ('*Dass es ist*'), the throwness (*Geworfenheit*) of being-there, the being historically placed and projecting itself *in the direction of the future* would correspond to Schelling's 'real existent', with the fundamental difference that Heidegger establishes, even starting from Kierkegaard, a system of being-there which therefore remains devoid of the Schellingian tension between a negative philosophy of reason and a positive philosophy of existence.

The existent that Schelling arrives at is instead the unconditionally Existent, or, in its full freedom to place itself, that which is before any thought and before any determination and therefore beyond any grounding. The task of positive philosophy is to find in the unconditionally existent what remains: the principle that 'stays' (*das Bleibende*) above all things, and this principle can only be the absolute original freedom. Vice versa, what Heidegger designates in *Being and Time* as *factum brutum* of the '*Dass es ist und zu sein hat*' ('that is and has to be') clearly alludes to a 'determined' field, even if in the sense of the *existential* of being-there and not of the Kantian categories.[10]

Although Heidegger here escapes (which underlines the great merit of his existential analytics) from the superimposition of a *Dass* with what expresses in the ontological-categorial context the factuality of the *Vorhandenheit* (of the simple presence, of the being available), nevertheless the *Dass* disclosed in the self-finding of the being-there (in the *Befindlichkeit* of the *Dasein*) must still be conceived 'as the existential determination [*Bestimmtheit*] of that entity [precisely of the *Dasein*] that is in the manner of the being-in-the-world'.

Heidegger goes on to point out that the *Befindlichkeit* of the being-there (the finding itself, the situation, which is always an emotional situation, harmonized) is not to be understood as an apodictic certainty deriving from perceiving oneself as reflective nor as an escape into irrationality:

> To expect to identify what the tonality has disclosed with what 'at the same time' the harmonised being-there knows, is aware of and believes, would mean totally ignoring the phenomenon of *what* it opens up and *how* it opens it up. Even when, in its belief, the being-there is 'sure' of its 'towards-where' or, rationally enlightened, thinks it knows something about its from where, none of it goes against the phenomenal state of fact, that tonality brings the being-there face to face with the fact-*that* of its *there*, which is fixed before it with its inexorable enigmaticity. From an existential-ontological point of view, there is no right to lower the 'evidence' of finding oneself, adapting it to the apodictic certainty of the theoretical knowledge of a mere available entity [*Vorhandenen*]. No less great, however, is *that other* falsification of these phenomena, which consists in relegating them to the *refugium peccatorum* of the irrational.[11]

The *self-finding* of the being-there has nothing to do with reflection, rather, '*Dasein* is always brought before itself, and has always found itself, not in the sense of coming across itself by perceiving itself, but in the sense of finding itself in the mood that it has',[12] that is, in an *affective situation* that constitutes it as a 'thrown projection'.

In *Sein und Zeit*, Heidegger describes a co-originality of self-finding (*Befindlichkeit*) and understanding (*Verstehen*). As being-within-the-world, being-there is in the world in the form of the projection (*Entwurf*), of the potency to be, of the opening to possibility, and it already and always has a certain (pre)understanding of a totality of meanings within which it moves. The being-there, as understanding, plans its being in possibility and the existential of the *Befindlichkeit* reveals that the 'projection' that constitutes the being-there is always a 'thrown projection'.

When Heidegger alludes to the double risk that is hidden behind the existential of the *Befindlichkeit* (understood as an emotional situation, that is, as harmonized self-finding) – on the one hand, in order to understand it in the sense of a sort of *a priori* that is found in the self-perception of some subject placed in the world, and, on the other, to reduce it, by virtue of the *Stimmung* that characterizes it, to an emotional environment, so to speak, that exceeds the rational – he shows, if nothing else, the limits that such a conceptual coupling inevitably brings with it. At the same time, however, he reveals the difficulties that manifest themselves at the threshold of the so-called ontological fracture opened, in my view, precisely with the theses expressed by Schelling in his *Philosophical Investigations* and followed by Heidegger, first on the terrain of the existential analytics of the *Dasein* and then, more coherently, on the ontological plane of being as event/appropriation (*Ereignis*). It is precisely this event, even with all the limits and possible (and dangerous for philosophical discourse) slips into a mystical-religious sphere, that is able to understand and express as a whole the question within which *one* moves from that abyssal awareness that also belongs to Schelling's *Mitwissenschaft*, or, to put it in the words of Meister Eckhart using the *Grund der Seele*, that is basically coincident with the 'unfounded grounding' of being in general.

2 Anxiety and the openness to being

Schelling's thought is present transversally and in a more or less conscious way in the various phases of Heidegger's philosophical journey, and it decisively accompanies the 'turn' following *Being and Time*. As Löwith argues, the facticity of the Heidegger of *Being and Time* seem to start from the 'positive' being of the later Schelling but, as the exchange with Jaspers shows, it cannot be argued in any way that Heidegger had Schelling's work in front of him as an indispensable point of reference at the time of writing. Rather, it is true that he found affinities and points of contact when writing the work that led him to deepen his knowledge of Schelling's philosophy. In particular, from the correspondence with Jaspers one can appreciate in an artificial way how Heidegger saw in the thought of the philosopher from Leonberg a theoretical closeness to the central themes of his reflection and, even more, a possible resource for the integration and overcoming of those positions, notoriously provisional, outlined in *Sein und Zeit*, such as to induce him to think of dedicating a seminar to *Philosophical Investigations* as early as 1927/8: in all probability an academic pretext to further his reading on a period in the history of thought that Heidegger considered decisive for his own theoretical path and more generally for the destiny of Western philosophy.

The need to study Schelling's crucial thought after *Being and Time* more deeply comes up again in another decisive phase of Heidegger's thought, namely in 1936, when he dedicated the famous *Vorlesung* to Schelling's work, precisely at a time when he was busy writing another work fundamental to his philosophical path, *Contributions to Philosophy* (which remained unpublished until 1989), and with which he attempted to clarify, after the 'turn', the meaning of being understood as *Ereignis* (event/appropriation). It should not be forgotten, of course, that in the background of such a theoretical development, the presence of reflection on the fundamental thoughts of Friedrich Nietzsche remains constant, an authentic 'filter' for understanding the notion of *Wollen* in Schelling, but above all a truly 'pivotal' author around whom the so-called Heideggerian 'turn' revolves.

It is clear that Heidegger's seminar in Marburg in 1927 was strongly influenced by the theses of his masterpiece *Sein und Zeit*, published that same year. What Hans Georg Gadamer, who studied in Marburg from 1919 to 1922 and again between 1924 and 1927 (finally obtaining his qualification in 1929), reports about that time is valuable. Although he mistakenly placed the seminar in 1925, before *Being and Time*, Gadamer tells how Heidegger insisted at length on a passage from *Philosophical Investigations*, in support of Schelling's greater theoretical depth compared to Hegel:

'The anxiety of life rips man from the centre' [Heidegger emphasized, quoting Schelling directly, adding]: you quote me a single passage from Hegel that equals this in depth![13]

The fact that Gadamer felt the need to report this Schelling quote, mentioned over and over again by Heidegger in class, helps to further highlight, where necessary, the centrality of the existential questions that were at the heart of the reflections in *Sein und Zeit* regarding Heidegger's approach to Schelling's *Philosophical Investigations*. The attention of the philosopher from Meßkirch is not directed by a vague and generic interest in the themes of German Idealism, within which Schelling's position assumes and overcomes the criticalities that emerge from an exclusively rationalistic approach. Rather, in his approach to *Philosophical Investigations*, Heidegger is strongly 'intentioned' by the analyses conducted in *Sein und Zeit*, indeed one could say that he is induced to verify its theoretical foundation in a text that is certainly central to the concept of Freedom, but more generally to the outcomes of the philosophical project of Modernity. The reference to *anxiety*, a theme just touched upon by Schelling in his *Philosophical Investigations*, yet central to a 1844 text by Kierkegaard (*The Concept of Anxiety*), strongly influenced by Schelling's thought and present in explicit quotation in § 40 of *Sein und Zeit*, underlines Heidegger's attempt to find an authoritative theoretical antecedent of reference for the *Angst* of his masterpiece. From this point of view, we can understand why this quote from Schelling, which certainly can still be found in the 1936 course, was imprinted in Gadamer's memory (who was nevertheless uncertain of its dating), albeit in an incidental and certainly insignificant way.

> The anxiety of life snatches man from the centre within which he was created; since this, like the pure essence of every will, destroys every personal will; to be able to live in it, man must die to all individuality, so it is almost necessary to leave the centre and search towards the periphery, to find in the latter a break for his own individuality.[14]

In anxiety, man (who is however to be understood as *pars pro toto*) feels his own groundlessness (as well as the nothingness of each finite entity), that is the absence of a certain grounding from which to think of his own being, and therefore is torn from his 'own' centre towards the periphery, in other words in open Conflict with the universal will within a 'free field of forces' (the space of the pure *Wollen*), which, as a non-grounding, *Indifference* of the Absolute, acts both as a necessary condition for existence and as an impossible grounding for existence itself. It is this *anxiety* that brings man before the original Freedom which, as Luigi Pareyson suggested, has the paradoxical characteristic of constituting itself as 'a grounding that always denies itself as such'.[15]

In this theoretical itinerary, the affinity with the theses of *Sein und Zeit* is affirmed, in which anxiety offers, so to speak, the phenomenal ground for the understanding of the original totality of being and of the being-there, but in the proposed juxtaposition one already glimpses the need for a step beyond the being-there in the direction of the being understood as *Ereignis* (event/appropriation). It is here that, as will be seen, the space described by a mere original *Wollen* can establish the condition of possibility for the actual 'giving of self' of the *Ereignis*.

As we have observed in the section dedicated to the major interpretations of the conceptual juncture represented by *Philosophical Investigations* and its theoretical consequences, Martin Heidegger seems to draft his existential analytics starting with the critical positions already reached by Schelling's reflection. In such a theoretical continuity, it is the same *anxiety* that acts as a link for the understanding of the passage from the ontic to the ontological.

> An understanding of Being belongs to *Dasein*'s ontological structure. As something that is [*Seiend*], it is disclosed to itself in its Being. The kind of Being which belongs to this disclosedness is constituted by state-of-mind and understanding [...]. As one of *Dasein*'s possibilities of Being, anxiety – together with *Dasein* itself as disclosed in it – provides the phenomenal basis for explicitly grasping *Dasein*'s primordial totality of Being. *Dasein*'s Being reveals itself as *care*.[16]

Anxiety, as a 'fundamental affective situation', is constituted as the opening/disclosing of the being-there. Unlike fear which has as reference something specific in front of which one feels fear, the 'in the face of which' of anxiety is completely indeterminate and this indeterminacy means the substantial irrelevance of any within-the-world entity: 'the world [as a whole] has the character of completely lacking significance'. In this sense, anxiety can open the being-there to the original totality of being, since it takes the possibility of 'understanding itself, as it falls, in terms of the "world"' away from the being-there and rejects the latter in its 'authentic potentiality-for-Being-in-the-world', to which a certain disorientation of the being-there is associated. From an ontological existential point of view, the not-being-at-home must, in fact, be conceived as the most original phenomenon.

> In man [Heidegger states in 1936, taking up Schelling's concept that clearly presents itself in a different language and context], the escape into selfishness is all the more pressing, since this selfish longing is the reason the will of the grounding, which tends to be obscure, wants to move away from the clarity of the luminous flash of the divine gaze [...]. The individual and separate will of man is threatened by this fire; it threatens to burn every individual will and every ipseity. The anxiety for his Self, the anxiety of life that is present in the depths of the being, pushes him away from the centre [...].
>
> The anxiety of life is a metaphysical necessity [...], it is an assumption of human greatness.[17]

The 'metaphysical necessity' that Heidegger speaks of is rooted in the fact that the 'in the face of which' of anxiety is basically the world itself as such. Already in § 40 of *Sein und Zeit*, the fundamental relationship between *anxiety* and the *Nothing* that would have been the central topic of the 1929 conference *Was ist Metaphysik?*, is clarified, a text that, as we have already mentioned and as we will see, represents a very important conceptual junction for the theoretical juxtaposition between Heidegger and Schelling that we are elaborating (including through Nietzsche's thought).

In the 1929 inaugural lecture, resuming the disorientation that accompanies anxiety as its primary effect, Heidegger argues that it brings us before the Nothing and that it makes the entity disappear in its entirety. Already in *Sein und Zeit*, again in § 40, Heidegger emphasized that in *anxiety* the world assumes the character of the most complete insignificance since 'anxiety "does not know" what that in the face of which it is anxious is', because what actually characterizes the '*in the face of which*' of anxiety is that the threatening something is nowhere. However, Heidegger continues:

> 'Nowhere', however, does not signify nothing: this is where any region lies, and there too lies any disclosedness of the world for essentially spatial Being-in.[18]

What in *Sein und Zeit* is clarified as 'the opening of *Dasein* for its authentic potency to be' will be defined from the 1929 inaugural lecture onwards as 'transcendence'. Already in *Sein und Zeit* the concept of *Nothing* that will be the object of *Was ist Metaphysik?* comes through, and which, I think, has an inseparable relationship with the ontology of the later Schelling. For now, however, let us limit ourselves to quoting a passage from § 40 whose theoretical content we will return to later:

> That in the face of which anxiety is anxious is nothing ready-to-hand within-the-world. But this 'nothing ready-to-hand', which only our everyday circumspective discourse understands, is not totally nothing. The 'nothing' of readiness-to-hand is grounded in the most primordial 'something' – in the *world*. Ontologically, however, the world belongs essentially to *Dasein*'s Being as Being-in-the-world. So if the 'nothing' – that is, the world as such – exhibits itself as that in the face of which one has anxiety, this means that *Being-in-the-world itself is that in the face of which anxiety is anxious*.[19]

That breach leading towards the 'turn' opens here in *Being and Time*, in the moment in which one realizes how, through anxiety, 'in the being-there of man there [comes] a state of mind capable of bringing him before the Nothing'.[20]

As we read in the 1929 conference, 'in anxiety the Nothing is encountered at one with beings as a whole'.[21] Through anxiety, therefore, the Nothing manifests itself 'not in such a way that the Nothing becomes manifest in our uncanniness [*Unverborgenheit*] quite 'apart from' beings as whole'.[22] So the Nothing manifests itself rather expressly with the entity and in the entity in so far as it disappears in its totality.

Thus, the problem of truth as unveiling or unconcealedness opens up, which for many of Heidegger's interpreters, including Pöggeler, Marx and Gadamer himself, signals and prepares the meaning of the 'turn' after *Being and Time*. On the other hand, it is precisely in the *Essence of Truth* from 1930 that for the first time there appears to be a 'turn' in Heidegger's thought, even if not yet in the sense of the reversal of *Time and Being* that leads to being as event by synthesizing the complete meaning of the turn.

In a way that is not so different, in Schelling, too, the nothingness of the entity is indicated by the call to the *Angst des Lebens* (anxiety of life) that alludes to the finite entities whose nothingness is affirmed by the selfish will of each entity that remains in itself in opposition to the Being of the Absolute that is reached through the universal will (or will to love) in which every single will is included. Here, too, Schelling's discourse on the nothingness of entities is to be understood as preliminary and preparatory to a general rethinking of being as time that follows the identification of the grounding with the original freedom.

3 The 'metaphysics of evil' and the 'metaphysics of the will': The 1936 course and the 1941 seminar

We will return later to the question of the openness of the being-there as transcendence and to the looming of a change of perspective that led Heidegger to the 'turn'. First, however, we must return to the comparison between Heidegger and Schelling, and to the insertion of the latter in a precise phase of the 'history of being'. As the course of 1936 amply demonstrates,

Heidegger arrives at Schelling's abyssal thought through consideration of Nietzsche's philosophical reflection and, in particular, through a 'modal' evaluation (which should, however, be defined as ante-predictive or ante-categorial) concerning the juxtaposition of Nietzsche's *Wille zur Macht* with the *Wirklichkeit*, actual reality, actuality. Heidegger strongly emphasizes the well-known expression in Schelling's *Philosophical Investigations* according to which the original being coincides with the will (*"Wollen ist Ursein"*), thus recalling to mind the absolute position of being as *Will to Power*, constantly present in the concluding trajectory of Nietzsche's philosophical thought, and in fact inserting Schelling in the same history of metaphysics that ends precisely with Nietzsche and thinks of being starting from presence.

Although Heidegger insists on Shelling's identification of the original being and of the will, seeing this overlap as relative to the merely ontic field, the understanding of the abyssal character of this expression, which in substance we find in the ontology of the *Will to Power*, passes through the fundamental consideration according to which the *Wollen* (the will) coincides *not* with the entity, but with the *original being* (with the *Ursein*), that is, not with what is real as an object and therefore as thinkable according to the Kantian categories of the *Critique of Pure Reason*, but rather as 'reality-actuality' absolutely placed and originally *in action*. In this sense, which is evidently antepredicative, we must accept Schelling's expression and the consequent theoretical juxtaposition with Nietzsche's *Wille zur Macht* that I propose as an alternative to the overlap that Heidegger suggests in relation to his reconstruction of the history of being.

It is certain that Heidegger's theoretical intention, already in the 1936 *Vorlesung* and in particular in the 1941 course dedicated to the *Metaphysics of German Idealism* and to the *Freiheitsschrift* as its theoretical peak, is aimed at finding confirmation of his assessment of the metaphysical concept of Western philosophy, for which, even in Schelling and Nietzsche (authors who in any case he saw as capable of providing the basis for reactivating a new beginning), the sense of being has been lost, or rather the oblivion of being has been consumed in favour of the mere consideration of the entities. This movement is particularly evident in the 1941 *Vorlesung*.

Compared to the 1936 course, the 1941 *Vorlesung* on the *Metaphysics of German Idealism* – published as volume 49 of the *Gesamtausgabe* and partly in the edition edited by Feick, probably choosing the most significant passages in agreement with the elderly Heidegger – presents continuity and points in common as well as substantial differences, which are useful, on the one hand, to highlight the complexity of Heidegger's Schellingian exegesis and, on the other hand, to show the fundamental characteristics of the philosophical reflection of the thinker from Meßkirch in its evolution.

In general, the 1941 course was aimed at inserting Schelling's theses on Freedom into the 'history of being', reading the *Wollen* (will) placed in the *Ursein* as the 'root' (*Wurzel*) of the ontological distinction of the *Wesen* in existence and grounding and, in the end, as the principle of a 'metaphysics of will', which would then reach its peak within the history of being precisely with Nietzsche's *Wille zur Macht*. To simplify this passage, we can say that if the 1936 *Vorlesung* was aimed at summarizing the philosophical project of the *Freiheitsschrift* in the (reductive) definition of a 'metaphysics of evil', then with the 1941 course, Heidegger definitively describes Schelling's writing on freedom as a form of 'metaphysics of the will', insisting on *Wollen* (will) as a 'metaphysical principle' that essentially repeats the characters of the 'history of being', understood as that issue that begins and is structured on the basis of the oblivion of being in favour of the entity.

Specifically, in the 1941 course the problem of the *Unterscheidung* (distinction) of the *Wesen* remains central; however, by Heidegger's explicit indication, this distinction and the consequent concept of existence (*Existenzbegriff*) are no longer to be traced back to the concept of existence described in *Sein und Zeit*; rather, Schelling's Existence is to be read as an oscillation between the traditional (metaphysical, in the Heideggerian sense of the expression) concept of *existentia* and the concept of existence from Kierkegaard's philosophy and the philosophy of existence in general.[23] In

Heidegger's view, Schelling intends the *Sebstsein* (selfhood) of the entity in the sense of subjectivity or egotism, however, this does not mean that Schelling reduces the whole discourse to a reflection on the being of man, indeed he extends his analysis to the whole ambit of the real (*das Wirkliches*).

In continuity with the 'traditional' concept of *existentia*, Schelling would, however, according to Heidegger, develop his *Existenzbegriff* within the history that thinks of being starting from the entity as existent. He would therefore not reach the antepredicative *Wirklichkeit* that I intend to place at the centre of my discourse, and which I believe to be the real object of Schelling's speculation. Moreover, compared to 1936, in the 1941 course Heidegger insists more on the *Wollen* of *Philosophical Investigations*, describing it as the 'root' (*Wurzel*) of the ontological distinction,[24] thus underlining the role it plays in the impossible grounding of the *Un-grund*, without however further investigating the theme in the direction of Indifference as absolute *Wirklichkeit*, but rather restricting the discourse to the realm of the existing inasmuch as it exists on the basis of the removal, the oblivion of being.

Curiously, in his first 'public' approach to Schelling's *Philosophical Investigations* that is to say in the seminar held in Marburg in 1927/8 just after the publication of *Being and Time*, Heidegger pointed out with great attention the theme of the *Un-grund*. As we shall see, I think the content of this seminar is particularly valuable in terms of the path that I intend to trace, also because it seems to appear the idea that in the *Un-grund*, in the Indifference, lurks that supra-modal *Wirklichkeit* that restores the inexhausted becoming of being free from connotations of a metaphysical nature. It seems that this is a phase in which the 'history of being', that would then accompany his theoretical path, is not yet marked out and therefore the identification of Schelling as a metaphysician of the will has not yet been established by Heidegger's reading

The Heidegger of the 'history of being' is convinced that both Nietzsche's Will to Power and Schelling's *Wollen* are to be understood as metaphysical principles that signal the oblivion of being; however, Nietzsche's *Wille zur Macht* and Schelling's *Wollen* always go beyond the ontic sphere, describing rather the original *Wirklichkeit*, which in its absolute *Wirksamkeit* (effectiveness) is described as a 'mere will' without object or representation. The *Urständlichkeit* (original inobjectuality/subjectivity) of the *Wirklichkeit* translates into a will that is always in action, a will that escapes the psychological definitions that belong, yes, to the ontic and that accompanies the originality of being and its character that is always actual.

This is confirmed by Martin Heidegger's speculation, and one understands how the *Ereignis* can, indeed must (under pain of exile to a mystical environment), be connected to the activity/actuality of Schelling's *unprethinkable being* (which is to be understood as the direct heir to the *Un-grund* of *Philosophical Investigations*) and to Nietzsche's Will to Power in its original *Dionysian* moment. What Heidegger writes in his *Nietzsche* about the *Wirklichkeit* and its connection to the will is enlightening:

Being – actual reality (*Wirklichkeit*, actuality) – will.
Being as an actual reality – actual reality as will.
Will – as a realising itself that aspires to itself according to a representing itself (the will of will).
(All this is essentially present, rejected to itself, in the clearing of being).
Will becomes essential in the *actualitas* only where the *ens actu* is determined by the *agere* as *cogitare*, since the latter is *cogito me cogitare*, be-self-aware (*Selbst-bewusst-sein*), where being aware as awareness (*Wissendheit*) is essentially the provide-self (*das sich-zu-Stellen*). […]
The will has never had, as its own (*zu eigen*), the beginning, it has already always essentially abandoned it with the forgetting.
The deepest forgetfulness is the non-remembering.[25]

In line with his 'history of being', Heidegger essentially identifies the will with a sort of metaphysical principle that constitutes the *Wirklichkeit* from within, assigning it a *dynamis* able to determine the existing and the thought on the existing insomuch as it is present. He certainly notes that in the will itself there is the tension to 'free itself' from its consist of as an 'essential and fundamental trait of beingness' and of the thought about it, but the will does not recognize itself as the 'essence of the truth' of being and in this ignorance lies, in Heidegger's opinion, the origin of the dominion over the existing.

The metaphysical superimposition proposed by Heidegger between the *Wirklichkeit* and the will is based, however, on an original removal (oblivion) by virtue of which the will 'has always abandoned' the *beginning*, that is to say the ontological sphere as the sum condition of possibility for the being and for the truth of the being. This very beginning that in my opinion Schelling determines as *Un-grund* first and as *unvordenkliches Seyn* second is the 'real', actual, never consumable, antepredicative residue of a supreme *Wirklichkeit* that Schelling describes in Berlin as *potentia potentiae* and therefore as pure space for a *Wollen* as a mere dynamic possibility.

The theoretical approach proposed by Heidegger comes through the analysis of the common abyssal grounding of being that both Schelling and Nietzsche describe as Pure Will. *Wollen ist Ursein*, writes Schelling in his *Philosophical Investigations* of 1809; and in this consideration, Heidegger can present Schelling as the authentic precursor to an interpretation of the theory of will and freedom that in Nietzsche found its radicalization and therefore the promise of a post-metaphysical philosophizing. In Heidegger's opinion, this identification of the original being with Pure Will consists in the first form of a true 'metaphysics of evil'. The theoretical context of the Heidegger of those years is strongly oriented towards the so-called turn and chronologically, too, the 1936 *Vorlesung* accompanies the drafting of the *Beiträge zur Philosophie* and therefore the definition of (which actually remains as an attempt at) a philosophy that identifies being with the *Ereignis*. In this sense, one cannot read Heidegger's evaluations of Schelling's thought as they are detached from his philosophical thought and theoretical articulation, especially since Heidegger's so-called history of philosophy is constantly 'bent' by the speculative intentions of the philosopher from Meßkirch (examples are the discussions about ancient thought, but more particularly the development of the interpretation of Nietzsche's thought that significantly accompanies the theoretical developments of the 'turn'). It is from this point of view that one understands the meaning to be assigned to Schelling's so-called metaphysics of evil, which Heidegger describes in *Wegmarken* as 'that philosophy which, when speaking of being, understands the entity as an entity'.

In Schelling's particular position it would be evident, in Heidegger's opinion, that the 'metaphysics of evil', as the foundation of a System of Liberty, is substantially directed at the fundamental forgetfulness/oblivion of the origin of being. Schelling therefore shows a Subject who, as an original will, fundamental and pure will, is strengthened to the point of making of itself (who is a Nothing) something. Such an action does not find an effective *Grund*, but rather an *Urwille* (an original will), in its absolutely actual role, but in itself completely inobjective (*urständlicher*), which as we shall see is very similar to (and, as already suggested by Luigi Pareyson, should therefore be read in connection with) the *Nichts* of the 1929 Heidegger conference *Was ist Metaphysik?*.

This abyssal (*abgründlicher*) grounding act was therefore a forgotten origin and therefore the *beginning of* a nihilistic thought that speaks of being but intending the entity as an entity. According to Heidegger, the forgetfulness of being is the fundamental thought of Western philosophy and Schelling's *Philosophical Investigations*, and the problematic conclusions it leads to represent the first critical 'emergence' of a removed and forgotten origin in the history of philosophical thought, which therefore declines in a nihilistic sense from its beginnings.

In Schelling's *Philosophical Investigations* – which, as Heidegger observes, although it discusses good and evil for man, does not have free will as its central theme, but instead the more general, ontological problem of freedom as the real grounding of being – evil is described as the insurrection of the perversion of the grounding of freedom. This perversion is made possible on the basis of the original distinction, which is presented as a constituent of each existing, between the essence insofar as it is the grounding and the essence insofar as it is existence.

As Heidegger observes in *Nietzsche*, in the section 'Sketches for the History of Being as Metaphysics':

> Schelling's distinction means a mutual opposition (struggle) that governs and structures the whole being essentially present (the entity in its beingness), and all this on the grounding of subjectivity.[26]

The struggle that Heidegger talks about here is the unresolved and unsolvable Conflict that presides over the grounding of the original Freedom because this is to be understood as the unique essence of a subjectivity never objectifiable, inobjective (*Urständlichkeit*), finally as absolute Actuality (*Wirklichkeit*, dynamically and allegorically described by the pure *Wollen*). It is the dynamic opposition between the particular will of the grounding and the general will of love, which, as mentioned, cannot be said to have been overcome once and for all, since it constitutes the very essence of Freedom, in other words the unsolvable essential Conflict that animates the entire ontological structure presented in *Philosophical Investigations*: that is, the *superior opposition* between necessity and freedom, that essential Conflict, without experience of which there cannot be philosophy.

Not even love, as the (always temporary) unification of the distinct principles of the *Seynsfuge*, can ever constitute the definitive victory of that Conflict which in truth constitutes the open space of Freedom. An unprethinkable space, never solvable in the intellect, that is configured (in order to make it 'humanly comprehensible') as *Wollen* (will), and that is to be read simply as *the necessary condition for the dynamic development* of the *ontological process* and *not as a metaphysical principle from which to deduce the possible manifestations of the All*.

4 *Un-grund* before the 'history of being': Seminar of 1927/8

As I have already mentioned, the reflections of the 1927/8 seminar on *Un-grund* are significant for the theses I am advocating, since the overlap with pure *Wollen* refers to an original dynamic that accompanies the being in all its manifestations in a phase of Heidegger's thought where Schelling's Will is not yet immediately brought back to a metaphysical principle in order to insert his thought within the 'history of being'.

The seminar that Heidegger held in Marburg between November 1927 and February 1928 was divided into nine lectures: the first four were expressly dedicated to Schelling's *Freiheitsschrift*; the other five to the exposition of a report by the attending students and the related discussion on the theme of freedom in authors such as Augustine, Meister Eckhart, Luther, Leibniz and Kant.

Another fundamental document for the understanding of the Heidegger-Schelling relationship is certainly Heidegger's notes on and accounts of the lectures from the first four days of the seminar (even if in reality there is no transcript for the first day). The *Nachschriften* of the attenders and the *Notizen* written by Heidegger are basically the first direct and public comparison between the philosopher from Meßkirch and Schelling's *Philosophical Investigations*. As we have already observed, the seminar days dedicated to the treatise on freedom start directly with the theme of the ontological distinction between essence as existence and essence as grounding, thus skipping the introductory issues relating to the possibility of a System of knowledge based on Freedom, a theme that, as we know, will be central to Heidegger's 1936 course.

On the second day of the seminar (7 December 1927), particular attention is paid to the ontological-anthropomorphic structure that underlies the above distinction and is substantially based on a 'metaphysics of the will', which we will need to return to later.

The notes relating to the third day of the seminar report the concepts of *Indifference* and *Un-grund*, which Heidegger tends to trace back to the structure of man's *Dasein*, as the central themes of the discussion on the ontological distinction, described the previous day. Also on this day, the theme of 'evil' and the aforementioned theme of the *Angst des Lebens* (anxiety of life) are also addressed, with their important repercussions for Heidegger's speculations following *Sein und Zeit*. At the end of the day, the fundamental lines for a possible 'philosophy of history' are mentioned within Schelling's concept that already unfolds in *Philosophical Investigations* and that leads to the future separation into positive and negative philosophy.

On the last seminar day that we are interested in considering, the importance of Schelling's *Freiheitsschrift* is considered, both for the overall understanding of the Leonberg philosopher's work and for the entire philosophical project of German Idealism. In particular, the meaning that the concept of being in general has in the *Freiheitsschrift* is analysed, first of all clarifying the relationship between duality and contrast (*Gegensatz*) and showing the concept of an *Offenbarwerden im Gegensatz* (of a being-revealed in contrast), according to which every essence (*Wesen*) can only reveal itself in its opposite. Also on this day (dated 11 January 1928 in the transcript), the concept of Love (*Liebe*) is brought back to that of the *Un-grund*, through the aforementioned explication of the possibility of the revelation in contrast. Lastly, the theme of creation and the consequent concept of time are traced.

The seminar of 1927/8 cannot be seen as a unified and systematic interpretation of the *Freiheitsschrift*, nor as a reading of a 'metaphysics of evil' or a 'metaphysics of will', unlike the 1936 Vorlesung. However, even this latter is a simplistic reading, since it does not entirely penetrate what Heidegger had intended it to be. Nevertheless, in the 'history of the effects' (with its necessary simplifications) the 1936 Vorlesung has certainly been preserved as the main legacy of Heidegger's interpretation, in which he read Schelling as a metaphysician of the will.

On the other hand, Schelling's anthropomorphism is highlighted by Heidegger in both the 1936 course and in the 1927/8 seminar. As I have already said, in terms of content, the main differences from the 1936 course lie firstly in the fact that in the 1927/8 seminar, Heidegger omits to consider the introduction and the related question of a possible System of Freedom, in order to immediately direct the investigation of the ontological distinction between *Wesen* as it exists and *Wesen* as grounding. Secondly – and here we most likely come to the core of the question – in the 1927/8 seminar the theme of *Un-grund*[27] is widely discussed also in relation to pure *Wollen* (will). First of all, *Un-grund* is used to clarify the unity of the *Seynsfuge* (juncture of being), then (on the third day) it is introduced as the grounding of the *Erregung* (excitement, agitation) of evil and, finally, it is read in union and contrast with *Liebe* (Love), for the clarification of Schelling's concept of Being.

The *Notizen* regarding the *Freiheitsschrift* transcribed by Heidegger in 1927 – which together with the transcriptions of the seminar days and the five reports of the participants contribute to complete the material relating to the *Schelling-Seminar* of 1927/8 – begin, significantly, with the phrase repeatedly underlined by Heidegger in his interpretation of Schelling's thought: '*Wollen ist Ursein*' (will is the original being). This sentence, which in the context in question precedes the ontological distinction of *Wesen* and which clearly we also generally consider decisive (if well understood and not hastily assumed as the founding thesis for a form of 'metaphysics of the will'), both in terms of the understanding of the theoretical course of the *Freiheitsschrift* and in terms of the meaning that it assumes for German Idealism, and more generally for Western philosophy, seems to be the real misunderstanding around which – according to most critics – Heidegger's interpretation orbits, and from which would arise the misunderstandings that end up leading Schelling's work to an escape towards irrationalism.

It is perhaps not too rash to assume that Heidegger's emphasis on the theme of *Wollen* (will) as an original being derives from the influence exerted at the time, and indeed for his entire speculative path, by Nietzsche's thought and in particular by the concept of *Wille zur Macht*. If read in this sense, Heidegger's emphasis takes on, in my view, a different light and is (in some ways surprisingly) more capable of penetrating into the deep meaning that *Wollen* has for the Schelling of *Philosophical Investigations* in connection with *becoming*: the true junction of the ontology of the *Freiheitsschrift*.

We will also see how in this Seminar of 1927/8 the concept of *Indifference*, or rather, of *Un-grund* (non-grounding) is directly aligned to the pure *Wollen* through a philosophy of *Nature* understood as the absolute position of self on a path that, from the banal and reductive anthropomorphism (although in some ways indisputably central in *Philosophical Investigations*), takes up the idea of an organic Nature that places itself, and organizes itself, in the becoming, starting from an impulse, from a spark, from a spark of life (*Lebensblick*), that Schelling coincides with original will (or rather with God's original will to self-reveal).

Heidegger also dealt with the theme of the *Un-grund* in the 1936 course, but this analysis is more meaningful in the 1927/8 seminar. In the 1936 *Vorlesung*, Heidegger came to delineate the characteristics of the *Un-grund*, as absolute *Indifference*, immediately after taking up the theme of the *Sehnsucht* as the essence of the grounding in God, that is, as 'the desire that the eternal One feels to generate himself'. Showing how the essence of God is fundamentally a becoming, Schelling supports his argument through the introduction of a pure will 'to make this being [the grounding in God] humanly comprehensible'. The pure will thus introduced, a will without intellect, which nevertheless moves in the direction of intellect and existence, founds and ensures the eternal becoming of God, indeed Heidegger states: 'The being-grounding of God is a modality of the eternal becoming of all God. And this becoming does not have its beginning in the grounding, but co-originally in the existence, that is, it is a becoming without beginning.' This becoming without a beginning that is co-originally in the existence and in the grounding can therefore only be founded in the non-grounding:

> The essence of being-God is a becoming [...]. Schelling's exposition gives the impression that God is at the beginning only *as a grounding*; but God is always that which is determined by grounding and existence, the original being which, as such, is its essence *before* any grounding and *before* any existent, and therefore in general before any duality. Schelling calls it *Urgrund* or rather *Ungrund* (non-grounding) – the *absolute indifference* of which no difference, not even the juncture of Being, can be properly

enunciated as a convenient predicate. The only predicate of the Absolute is the absence of a predicate, without the Absolute becoming a nothing with it.[28]

As is well known, for Schelling the grounding of the becoming in God justifies and sustains the becoming of things outside of Him, so that the very being of things is, in the end, *becoming*. This becoming has nothing to do with a simple phenomenological observation according to which in the world we never witness the stagnation of an immutable being. Quite the contrary; this concept of becoming is grafted rather into the overall framework of a *dynamic* Absolute such as Schelling was elaborating in the middle of his philosophy of Identity, also by virtue of his (multiform and controversial) 'doctrine' of the powers. As Heidegger himself observes, that the being of things is a becoming means:

> That things are [that is, they exist, they come into existence], but the essence of their Being consists in presenting each time a degree and a mode in which the Absolute pro-pounds and ex-pounds itself in a determined way. Being is not dissolved in a superficial liquefaction called becoming, on the contrary, becoming is conceived as a mode of Being. But now the Being is originally conceived as will. The entity is existing according to the disposition (*Fügung*) in a willing of the moments of the grounding and existence, belonging to the juncture of the Being. The Being of things is a becoming: this means that the existing things aspire to certain degrees of will each time; in their domain there is never the indifferent uniformity of a simply present multiplicity.[29]

The degrees and modalities in which the Absolute manifests itself (pro-poses itself/ex-pounds itself) are therefore determined by a pure will that Heidegger limits himself to describing again in the forms of a metaphysical principle, but which is to be understood as a *free conflict of forces that tend towards the form* (towards the manifestation of the Absolute in the *ek-sistere* [exist]) in the presence, towards its conservation, its strengthening and therefore towards the suppression of the form itself in favour of the subsequent form (manifestation). That Heidegger tends to include Schelling's thought in a sort of 'metaphysics of the will' (which seeks to hold together being and becoming) similar to that which the Meßkirch thinker himself mistakenly attributes to Nietzsche is testified to in the following passage:

> Here Schelling approaches, without really taking possession of it, the true metaphysical relation between Being and becoming, which have always easily escaped the gaze of thought, because it is lost in formal conceptual relations between the two representations; not even Nietzsche escaped the traps of formal dialectics on this point.[30]

The fact that the alignment suggested by Heidegger is based on a general misrepresentation of the concept of will in the two authors does not authorize the abandonment of the evocative parallel, on the contrary, it urges, in my opinion, a reconstitution of it on the basis of an investigation into the real meaning that the will assumes in Schelling and Nietzsche. The possibility of escaping the 'traps of formal dialectics' may be found in a correct reading of the dynamics of the *Wille zur Macht* (which we have tried at least in part to retrace in *Will to Love*), or in a correct reading of the will in Schelling's *Philosophical Investigations* that, taking into account the overall path of the philosopher, traces the will itself to the *real activity* and the conflict of forces that act in the depths of Nature, ontologically before any possible thought about being.

I think I can say that the latter aspect was in fact probed by Heidegger in the *Schelling-Seminar* of 1927/8, in an interpretation that is certainly more faithful to Schelling's thought than the contents of the 1936 *Vorlesung* appear to be, largely theoretically conditioned by the evolution of Heidegger's thought.

During the third of the seminar days of 1927/8, Heidegger goes over the question of the *Un-grund* in relation to the ontological distinction between the essence, inasmuch as it exists, and the essence, inasmuch as it is grounding, underlining, though without an explicit reference to the philosophy of Identity, how this distinction is based on an *Indifference* (non-difference) that ontologically precedes any distinction: a principle that will still be the basis for the distinction of the *Urwesen* from the *Stuttgart Private Lectures*.

Such Indifference (which, as said, derives from the concept of Identity as 'Identity of identity and difference', as a bond of the bond) is however only possible within a concept of being as becoming:

> The way of the original essence of the *Ungrund* is the *becoming* – in the sense that the essence is always becoming.
>
> The determination of being in this *Ungrund* as essence (*Wesen*) cannot be only what befits it as existence, nor what befits it as grounding, but what befits it as *its* essence (*Wesen*).[31]

Immediately after, according to what emerges from Friedrich's transcription, and in order to describe the characteristic of the *Un-grund*, Heidegger uses the outdated verb '*wesen*', which actually means 'exist, being essentially' and that to a certain extent underlines how such a way of 'existing' clearly goes beyond being as presence and addresses rather the Being of the Absolute (being that in Schelling's meaning maintains a *transitive* meaning, through which the Absolute, considered *par excellence, commands* the being in the copula of judgement for what of the Absolute manifests itself):

> The *Ungrund* [states Heidegger] *west* (it exists, it is essentially) insomuch as it is whole in each of them [existence and grounding], therefore they – without being different – cannot both be *present* in it at the same time.[32]

This characterization of the *Un-grund*, however, requires a (*dynamic*) principle that shifts from Indifference and leads to distinction. Since, according to Heidegger, the possibility of evil resides in the original ontological distinction, the doctrine of the *Un-grund* clearly becomes central to this dynamic. 'In the *Ursein* (original being)', Heidegger states, 'there is a total in-distinction (*Ungeschiedenheit*). For the happening (*Geschehen*) a solicitation is needed. How can this solicitation be? Why, in general, must the Indifference, the in-distinction of the non-grounding (*Un-grund*) (*Ur-grund*, original grounding), be removed (aufgehoben)?'³³ Schelling responds, as we know, by introducing God's will to self-revelation as an impulse of the agitation of the state of *Indifference*. The profound reason suggested by Schelling was that God cannot remain in indecision because in general in creation nothing can remain uncertain, ambiguous. It seems, however, that Schelling believes that not even God himself is able to escape from this ambiguity (*Zweideutigkeit*) without a 'general basis of solicitation', of tendency to evil, if only to bring the two principles to life in him. That basis is identified by Schelling with the *Nature* in him. In considering this passage from *Philosophical Investigations*, Heidegger pauses to analyse the logical process that Schelling follows in order to argue about the need for this primary solicitation that shifts from *Indifference*.

Heidegger is critical of Schelling because he doubts that the ambiguity present at the grounding of *Indifference* is valid as a condition for the necessary solicitation and for the consequent 'existence' of the two principles:

> The 'just as-so too' is an expression for ambiguity, so that Schelling seems to define the *Ungrund* just as he refuses to define it. If everything has disappeared, dissolved, then the expression 'neither-nor' is valid; in it, however, still resides a *last* look back at the 'disappearance', at the 'dissolving'. In the case of ambiguity, it is not really possible to speak of an absolute 'disappearance'. Schelling here does not accurately distinguish between 'just as-so too' and 'neither-nor', and in this doubling (*Doppelung*) within the *Ungrund* in the sense of 'disappeared', 'dissolved', but equally still disturbing, there is a certain right to speak of 'ambiguity' of that essence, which is the original being (*Ur-sein*), namely the will (*Wollen*), the impulse (*Drang*).³⁴

The Heideggerian criticism of Schelling's argument is not so much aimed at underlining the logical-formal deficiencies of his discourse, but rather at highlighting how these deficiencies can be traced back to the theme that Schelling seems to want to revisit here on a 'logical' level. The difficulties encountered by Schelling's argument are essentially rooted in the fact that *Un-grund* is to be understood not only as a space of possibility for the original ontological distinction but also as a (*dynamic*) principle of a particular form of philosophy of Nature, which cannot be solved in an exclusively physical-mathematical vision, but rather requires a broader organic concept, in which it recognizes its *Selbstheit* (its selfhood, its aseity) and – much more importantly, from my point of view – the fact that its *absolute Setzung* (absolute position) always remains something impenetrable to knowledge, 'something positive – at the same time a dynamic principle, an impulse – that has space for action and has decided by itself exactly how it shows itself in the concrete instance'.

As can be seen from the same reading conducted by Heidegger in this important seminar of 1927/8, the anthropomorphism that certainly guides the progress of *Philosophical Investigations* is not in itself sufficient to clarify in its entirety the discourse of ontological freedom, which has its roots not in the analogy with human freedom, as a property of the individual, but in the organic and complex constitution of a Nature that has always preceded the spiritual sphere (intelligible) as an original and persistent (*bleibende*) impulse, produced by multiple forces, that Schelling designates with the general term of 'will' only to make the process 'humanly comprehensible'.

Schelling's sentence according to which the relationship between grounding and existence in God 'is not a System but a life' is understood in an anthropomorphic key only if it is connected to a more general concept that involves the organic constitution of Nature, and the very idea of will as a property of the individual or as a metaphysical principle, is overcome by the idea of 'a band of living forces' that are unified and distinguished:

> The will of man is to be considered as a band of living forces [*ein Band von lebendigen Kräfte*]: now, as long as it itself remains in its unity with the universal will, even those forces remain in divine measure and balance. But as soon as the individual will itself has moved away from the centre that is its place, the bond between the forces also disappears; in its place dominates a mere particular will, which can no longer unify the forces under it, such as the original will, and that therefore must tend to form or put together its

own separate life with the forces detached from each other, with the rebel army of appetites and desires (since each individual force is also a passion and a desire), which is only possible because even in evil there continues to be the primitive bond [*das erste Band*] of forces, the grounding of nature. But since, however, there can be no real life, beyond what could only result from the original connection, so arises a single life, but false, a life of lies, a germination of restlessness and destruction.³⁵

The dynamics present in the original being described by Schelling through the 'humanly more comprehensible' concept of will (*Wille*) emerge not only in the 1927/8 seminar (which also for this reason seems to be much more faithful to Schelling's writings than the subsequent references by Heidegger to *Philosophical Investigations*) but also in the 1936 *Vorlesung*, albeit in a rather incidental way in a passage that we have already mentioned:

> Schelling in fact does not think 'concepts', he thinks forces and thinks positions of will, he thinks in the conflict of powers that cannot be agreed by means of a conceptual artifice.³⁶

As Iain Hamilton Grant pointed out in his 2006 book *Philosophies of Nature after Schelling*, the freedom of the 1809 *Philosophical Investigations* is essentially rooted in the ontological primacy assigned to Nature, in whose organic structure *forces* act that assume the vestiges of a will, whether universal or individual, in an unstoppable conflict of powers that can never be reconciled by means of conceptual structures (see in particular I. H. Grant, *Philosophies of Nature after Schelling*, London: Continuum, 2006, 187 ff.). Moreover, in the 1927/8 seminar, Heidegger describes the dialectic summarized in the contrast between a universal will and a particular will as a conflict between the polarity of the impulse (*Polarität des Dranges*),³⁷ according to an expression that is more suited to a field of natural forces than to a merely moral sphere.

It has been seen that for Schelling, to shift man from his own in-distinction, that is, from his Indifference, the *anxiety of life* that Heidegger wanted to emphasize with such conviction even in the attempt to establish a link with the anxiety of *Sein und Zeit*, enters into the equation. On the third day of the seminar, the anxiety of life is presented immediately after Heidegger's reflection on the *Un-grund* and on the rooting of ontological Freedom in the forces of Nature. This confirms the progress of *Philosophical Investigations*, which undoubtedly relies constantly on an anthropomorphic reading without, as I said, being able to reduce itself to it completely. Heidegger himself, in fact, emphasizes how the anxiety of life as an impulse of the agitation of the state of Indifference, does not have a 'logical-dialectic character', and how Schelling himself reads in it 'the powers of its own existence, in which he saw certain perspectives of which he offered the general ontological grounding without, however, grounding it universally'.[38] The impossibility of *dialectically founding* the exit from the state of Indifference depends exclusively on the fact that the vision that Schelling proposes here essentially requires a *dynamic* being, that is to say a *becoming* on the basis of which he can, however, hypothesize a particular form of 'philosophy of history' that he will try – without succeeding – to develop in the *Weltalter* and that in any case will lead to the distinction between a negative philosophy and a positive philosophy, which, as Heidegger himself noted in 1927, seems to be widely prefigured already in the theses of the 1809 *Philosophical Investigations*. In fact, the principle of evil, which is possible in the distinction between the essence inasmuch as it exists and the essence inasmuch as it is the grounding, provokes and determines in opposition to itself the 'birth of the Spirit, which is the sphere of history'. At the end of the third day of the seminar, Heidegger draws the distinction between negative philosophy and positive philosophy, with the idea that in Schelling history is understood as starting from a metaphysical consideration: by negative philosophy 'Schelling means the metaphysical consideration of the totality of the existing, which includes first of all a universal ontology of the existing in general and therefore also in a separate sphere'.[39] With the expression positive philosophy Schelling designates 'the meaning of the existing itself in its singularity, uniqueness (*Einmaligkeit*) both in Nature and in history as a unitary process, which is built in certain stages'.⁴⁰ As we can see, already at this time Heidegger read positive philosophy and negative philosophy in an inseparable relationship, in which they were mutually necessary to each other.

As we mentioned when illustrating the themes on which this first reading of *Philosophical Investigation* dwells, Heidegger sees in this work both the crucial point of Schelling's speculation through which it is possible to deduce, on the one hand, the theoretical origins and, on the other, the subsequent developments and – much more significantly – the critical position of the central problems of German Idealism in general. Specifically, Heidegger is keen to underline how Schelling arrives at, through the *Freiheitsschrift* (and the subsequent distinction into negative and positive philosophy), the same problem that is in Hegel's *Logic*, namely

> How a universal ontology must necessarily be oriented with respect to the determined being, to man himself, who must also have an ontic function.⁴¹

The solution attempted by Schelling (also on the basis of the reading of the teleological section of Kant's *Critique of Judgement* and of Plato's *Timaeus* and *Philebus* theses) is that of an overall organic System which, starting from an original ontological constitution such as an unstoppable Conflict of forces present in the Absolute considered *par excellence*, determines in its *dynamic* development (precisely according to the 'doctrine of powers') forms which preserve within them the same structural organization as a whole. Heidegger certainly did not achieve such a penetration of Schelling's System, nevertheless he brought to light the basic theoretical aspects that lead in that direction and although, particularly in the 1936 course, he was strongly conditioned by his own speculative plan which was to classify both Schelling's and Nietzsche's philosophies as 'metaphysics of the will', he could not help but notice how in Schelling's philosophy of Nature there are the conditions for a post-metaphysical philosophy that lead in the direction of a *dynamic ontology*, still only in outline and yet to be fully thought out.

The fourth seminar lecture of 1927/8 also carries on in this vein; here, in fact, the themes of creation and time are dealt with. In particular, it is worth dwelling on Heidegger's notes on the notion of time, since he sees in it the same ambiguity that characterizes the *Seinsbegriff* (concept of being).

The anthropomorphism of *Philosophical Investigations* leads Schelling to deal with the problem of time in relation to the generation of man in *time* and to his ontological in-distinction. In reality, the problem has a more general character, essentially ontological, which concerns the overall approach of *Philosophical Investigations*, in which the problem of Freedom (precisely ontological) is considered from the perspective of a philosophy of Identity where, in the above-mentioned over-relationship of identity, the sphere of Nature, as 'real position of self, an original and fundamental will that does something and is the grounding and basis of every essence' is ontologically placed before the Fichtean Ego that 'coincides with its own act and is awareness and position of self'.

The dynamic identity structure that constitutes each essence belongs all the more to man, who is initially, in the original creation, an undistinguished being, 'in a state of innocence and primitive bliss', who can nevertheless decide for himself through a decision, which however does not fall *into* time. Let us follow Schelling's argument.

> It [the decision] falls out of all time, and therefore coincides with the first creation albeit as an act distinct from it. Man, although generated over time, is nevertheless produced in the principle of creation (in the centre). The act by which his life is determined in time does not itself belong to time, but to eternity, it does not then precede life according to time, but through time (without being touched by it) as an action that is eternal by nature. For it, the life of man reaches the principle of creation: therefore, man, through himself, is also outside of the free creation and is himself an eternal principle.[42]

In this passage by Schelling, Heidegger sees a fundamental ambiguity about the concept of time that is rooted directly in the ambiguity of the concept of being

(*Seinsbegriff*), since, on the one hand (when referring to entities as present), it seems to coincide with the common concept of succession and, on the other, with the general power of the world. The organic idea of time ensures that each essence (including man, of course) has its own time and that, nevertheless, this concept can be configured, in creation, as a succession of moments. Just as we witness the double life in the Absolute, where each entity is, at the same time, for itself as a determined entity and in the Absolute considered *par excellence*, we also notice how the determined entity is such within a temporal structure commonly understood as succession and how at the same time its own time persists in it that is then the time of the Absolute. This concept, which appears as incompatible 'according to the common way of thinking', is based only on an organic-dynamic concept of the Absolute: 'therefore man, through himself, is also outside of creation [therefore outside of time as succession], free and is himself *eternal* principle', since he has his own time within himself and in any moment can separate himself from time as succession.

What we need to keep clear on our journey regarding this discourse is the fact that Heidegger stops to underline in Schelling the double concept of time in intimate affinity with the ambiguity belonging to the concept of being. In the 1936 *Vorlesung*, this aspect is not treated directly, but constitutes, on the one hand, the axis around which the reflection on the becoming of God and of creation revolves and, on the other, the basic ontological structure that supports the idea of a 'superior realism', as a companion, together with the ideal centre, to the philosophy of (dynamic) Identity that is based on the idea of an Absolute as *Gesamtorganismus* (overall organism).

In fact, it is on the basis of the ambiguity of the concept of time that Heidegger can describe the creation of *Philosophical Investigations* as 'happening, the coming-out-of-itself of the Absolute that comes to itself, motility within the essence of creation and, therefore, of the becoming and of the being of created nature'.[43] To represent the mediation – clearly not conceptual, but always and only dynamic – that allows creation, Schelling places the 'humanly comprehensible' (though in reality much more complex) concept of will, so that – as Heidegger observes – creation shows itself as 'a flexion of the eternal will of desire that bends to the will of the verb, to meditation; for this reason, creation itself is a will and a being that becomes in the will'.[44]

As said, a purely conceptual vision of Liberty, that is, an exclusively idealistic concept of Liberty, could certainly not be organically structured as the basis and grounding of a *dynamic ontology*, as attempted by Schelling; and it would at most have the capacity to found a freedom such as *Eigenschaft* (property as faculty) of the absolute Ego. On the contrary, Schelling organizes the discourse about the original Freedom on the basis of a philosophy of Identity (of Nature and Spirit) that assigns an ontological primacy to the natural sphere and of this Heidegger is absolutely aware both in the 1927 seminar and in the 1936 course, where he reiterates that Schelling contrasts in the (over-)relationship of identity to Idealism, as an interpretation of the being that understands the being-in-itself of the entity as freedom, a higher realism in which Nature is not simply configured as non-Ego but as a 'power that exists in itself' which is in reciprocal action with the ideal sphere (all this in accordance with that 'mutual interpenetration of realism and idealism that was the clarified goal' of Schelling's efforts[45]).

Preventing Heidegger from understanding the meaning of such an ontological structure, however, is the attempt to reduce (for reasons internal to the progress of Heidegger's philosophy) Schelling's 'will' to the course of the 'history of being' and in particular to Leibniz's concept that can be traced back to the identification of *perceptio et appetitus* (an attempt that Heidegger also makes, for more or less the same reasons, with regards to Nietzsche's *Wille zur Macht*). In this vein, the will is unduly and inevitably understood as a 'metaphysical principle' and Schelling's approach appears a simple overturning of classical Idealism, so that Nature assumes in the end aspects of Fichte's Ego in *its* will.

3

The unyielding excess of Being

1 Will and Being

If we were to briefly summarize the theoretical path travelled by Heidegger's philosophy over the years we would probably not err if we turned to what Heidegger himself said during a seminar held at Le Thor in 1969.[1] On that occasion Heidegger divided his theoretical journey into three phases, emphasizing a continuity that today, after careful reconsideration of his work, is almost unanimously recognized: (1) the first phase, when his efforts were directed at the central question of *Sein und Zeit* on the meaning of Being (*Sinn des Seins*); (2) the next phase when his investigation was influenced by the introduction of the question concerning the 'truth' of Being (seen, however, as the 'history of Being', beginning from the *Dasein* that poses the question); and (3) finally, in the third phase, where his philosophical work focused on tracing a sort of 'topology of Being' as a question concerning the place or location of Being.

The philosophical step that led Heidegger to the 'turn' with respect to the positions of *Sein und Zeit* lies in a change of perspective, which no longer begins from the Being of man in order to understand the meaning of Being in general, but speaks directly to the Being, or rather to the Becoming and the evolution of the 'history of Being' in which, nonetheless, man is not to be seen as a passive spectator nor as a mere tool of destiny. For Heidegger metaphysics, inasmuch as it is thought that considers the Being in its totality, does not translate into the distortion of this or that thinker of a given historical period; it is rather to be seen as a way of determining the Being itself, which directly involves humanity and at the same time is directly involved in the activities of man.

Within the 'history of Being' traced by Heidegger in the firm belief that this was based on the original oblivion of being (*Sein*) in favour of consideration of the Being[2] (as entity; *das Seiende*), the Metaphysics of German Idealism (meaning the philosophical project that intends to reduce the Being to the *will* of the subject – powerful and *knowing*), reaches its maximum expression in the principal philosophical works by Hegel and in particular in *Phänomenologie des Geistes* (*Phenomenology of Spirit*), where 'the essence of the transcendental consideration that reflects on the conditions of Being in nature and on the essence of the idea itself' is shown unconditionally. Nevertheless, Heidegger himself emphasizes that in Schelling's response to *Phänomenologie des Geistes*, that is to say in his 1809 *Philosophical Investigations into the Essence of Human Freedom*, Metaphysics of German Idealism, being the metaphysics of the 'unconditional representation' (which, according to Heidegger, is expressed once again in this crucial work through the tension of the *mere will* towards the intellect), appears more radically in the figure of the self-conscious Absolute, in its *becoming*, through 'voluntary reason'. In this dynamic, however, Heidegger sees a dangerous overlapping of the concept of Being as *Ereignis*, which had become the keyword of his philosophy since 1936, as he wrote in his *Letter on Humanism*. For Heidegger it was an immediate and rather interesting interweaving that he attempts to elude – as the Absolute was, for him, totally within the 'history of being' beyond which he intended to pose the *Ereignis* – although not very convincingly:

> The 'matter [*Sache*] itself' (which metaphysics is to think), [writes Heidegger in his seminar notes from 1941-1943, edited by Hildegard Feick

in the appendix to *Schellings Abhandlung*, and published in 1971], is 'the Absolute'. Because the Absolute is thought as unconditional subjectivity (that is, subject-objectivity), as the identity of identity and non-identity, and subjectivity essentially as will-full [*willentlich*] reason and thus as movement, it looks as if the Absolute and its motion coincided with what the thinking of the history of Being thinks as *Ereignis*. But *Ereignis* is neither the same as the Absolute nor is it even its contrary, for instance, finitude as opposed to infinity'.[3]

The position expressed by Heidegger is certainly instrumental to his philosophical perspective, which identifies in Being as *Ereignis* the *destiny* that reaches its zenith in the 'history of Being', beyond the consideration of Being as 'presence'. Nonetheless the distance from Schelling's Absolute, which Heidegger feels the need to mark so explicitly, is clearly based on a number of misunderstandings and simplifications of Schelling's philosophical perspective.

A careful reading of Schelling's Absolute can clarify the affinity not only with Heidegger's *Ereignis* – one of the focal points of contemporary philosophical thinking – and how this can (I would say *must*) in the end be seen in continuity with Schelling's Absolute, but also with the dynamics of Nietzsche's *Wille zur Macht* thanks to the definition that Heidegger presents of the *ontological difference* (between *das Sein* and *das Seiende*) and in support of a philosophical intuition that otherwise runs the risk of being seen only beyond the confines of philosophical thinking as the abandonment to a 'mystical' sphere, to a sort of negative theology.

I am convinced that the critical comparison of Schelling and Nietzsche, proposed by Heidegger in his 1936 *Vorlesung*, leads in the direction of a concept of absolute (ontological) freedom, as the original foundation of Being and the entity, and that in this sense Being, seen as *Ereignis*, prepares, on the one hand, to resume the indissoluble (coessential) bond with Time and, on the other, to avoid a concept that sees Being still and only beginning with the existent, rooted in the interpretation of the *pure will* that Heidegger reads, both in Schelling and in Nietzsche, in connection with the *Ursein* (primal Being).[4] This conceptual overlapping, however, is not to be understood – as Heidegger would wish – in the sense of a 'metaphysics of will' since this would mean assuming a 'will' that, subordinate to reason, finally coincides completely with it, restoring a metaphysical principle that can be deduced starting from the Being inasmuch as it is present. On the contrary, Schelling's perspective (like that of Nietzsche) offers a totally different concept of 'will', which, on the one hand, certainly translates into the rational form that sees the Being inasmuch as it is present (and in this responds perfectly to the philosophical project of Idealism and presents itself as a relative 'metaphysical principle') but, on the other hand – a truly qualifying aspect of Schelling's and later Nietzsche's *will* – presents itself as over-realistic *excess* that can never be totally consumed in Reality (as beings objectively present) and in the concepts related to Reality: that is to say as a resource of the rational form itself, or as the Principle that is permanent and (absolutely) free of Being. That is, in effect, the very object of Schelling's positive philosophy.

The possibility of seeing Being as *Ereignis* is already clear in Schelling's and Nietzsche's 'critical' conclusions and is essentially based on a concept of will that exceeds the idealistic attempts to saturate Reality (as *Wirklichkeit*) in the thought, that is in the concept of Reality itself. In Schelling, as in Nietzsche in fact, the will is never completely reduced to reason and forms of thought, nor can we speak of a will that coincides exactly with the 'will' of the 'unconditional representation'. The excess of will (effective, alogical) with respect to the rational form that aims to grasp Being inasmuch as it is existent shows itself in Schelling's and Nietzsche's thinking, in the 'gap' that for both of them could be seen at the zenith of the movement determined by will itself, that is at the peak of an apparent 'metaphysics of will'. At the extreme of metaphysical thinking, the exhaustion of the Ideal's capacity to saturate in its expressions the Inexhaustibility of Reality appears historically (*seynsgeschichtlich*) with the end of onto-theology: in Nietzsche, this determines the 'death of God' and in Schelling the inevitable division of philosophy into negative (or rational) and positive (or historical), a division that was already prepared by the introduction of the *Un-grund* (non-grounding) in *Philosophical Investigations*. From the Open space in the differences thus created, it was possible for the forgotten and denied original *Un-grund* to emerge, 'happening' historically (*seynsgeschichtlich*) in the thinking that can 'think' of being 'as' *Ereignis*.

In Schelling's Will to Love and Nietzsche's Will to Power (in what we could call its 'Dionysian' meaning), inasmuch as they are extreme manifestations of will, Being exceeds the being present and shows an inexhaustible origin from which every *destiny* of Being derives.

From this point of view, *Being as Ereignis* appears in its inevitable bond with Time, not as if the event were a manner of being, nor, vice versa, as if Being were a manner of the event, but only in the sense that the event is what 'makes happen' and what destines the Being (allowing it to be present), and what finally *offers* the time. Inasmuch as Being is event, the event is 'what makes happen', only this can be said of the event and of its inexhaustible origin without falling into the thinking that begins from a grounding (*Grund*): *Ereignis ereignet*, 'the event makes happen'. To understand Being in this way is to avoid the metaphysical fallout that confines our thinking to the form that perceives Being starting with a grounding, and above all it means opening oneself to the infinite freedom of being. Although Schelling did not present a completed published work after his *Philosophical Investigations*, this was due to the type of problem that he was working on, beginning with the treatise on freedom. Nietzsche, 'the only essential thinker after Schelling', also failed in his main work, *Will to Power*, for the same reasons. But this magnificent dual shipwreck of the great thinkers is not a failure and should not be considered negatively: quite the contrary. It is the rise of that which is totally other: the spark of a new beginning. Anyone who truly knows the reason for this shipwreck – affirms Heidegger – and, knowing it, overcomes it, should become the founder of a new beginning of Western philosophy.[5]

As we have already seen, Heidegger emphasizes – although, more or less speciously – how in Schelling's and Nietzsche's respective shipwrecks we can, or rather must, glimpse the spark of a possible *new Beginning (Anfang)* for Western philosophy, which we know could have been realized – for him – in the concept of *Ereignis*, he allows Schelling's Will and Nietzsche's Will to Power to coincide with the principle of the philosophical project of the Metaphysics of German Idealism. In this, the critical innovation of the two philosophers would be completely resolved and saturated, to the point that therefore it becomes impossible to understand which step forward they have taken – even in their *failure* – beyond the metaphysical project of Idealism and the 'history of Being' in general. By the same token, *mere will* placed in essential coincidence with *Ursein* – the primal Being which, inasmuch as it is *ontological excess*, is never wholly reduced to Being as present, nor to the conceptual form that it means to represent – bears witness to an ontological vision that binds together Being and Time in a *dynamics* freely regulated by a (necessarily no better-defined) *will*, that acts as the inevitable and permanent Principle for the entire structure and conservation of the Absolute in its Becoming. With respect to the complete saturation of Reality – foreshadowed as the metaphysics of Idealism in the form of a knowledge that proceeds according to an unconditional will to represent – in Schelling's criticism of Idealism (which as we know always preserves a lively realism in its grounding) and in Nietzsche's ontological concept of *Wille zur Macht* (which is also firmly anchored to the absolute position of Being as eternal becoming), beyond the rational form to which Being delivers itself, the unresolvable *excess* of an alogical setting, which always precedes the concept and which is configured as mere *will*, is clearly evident.

What we intend to show here is that metaphysics, in the Heideggerian sense of the 'history of Being' which thinks and structures Being beginning from the consideration of the being as entity, and thinks of every form of Being as always starting with a grounding (in the sense of philosophy as *onto-theology*),[6] certainly reaches completion in the nihilism of the Nietzschean vision, but this fateful landing place which allows us to see Being, beyond the grounding, as *Ereignis*, is already to be seen in the alogical *excess* that Schelling sees as ontological freedom, that is the impossible grounding (*Un-grund*) of Being[7].

This indomitable *excess*, this *previously inconceivable* (unprethinkable: *unvordenklich*) lack of grounding (*Un-grund*) of Being, must not be seen exclusively as a fixed and immobile residue. For Heidegger, at the zenith of metaphysics, the 'history of Being' finally, in the philosophical project of German Idealism, coincides with the will, which in Fichte, Schelling and Hegel is translated into the unconditional will to represent Reality in the concepts of reason. Nevertheless, in *Philosophical Investigations into the Essence of Human Freedom*, Schelling identifies Pure Will as the primal Being (*Ursein*) and at the same time introduces a non-grounding (*Un-grund*) into the differentiation, without predicates ('although not a nothingness or an inconsistent'), which nonetheless foresees the forms of Being inasmuch as it is existent. This non-grounding, absolutely in place, the atopical place of the perfect *Indifference*, constitutes the possibility of the possibility of Being, that is to say the *potentia potentiae* of Being, and is thus traced back to what Schelling calls the 'pure will' of the *Grund*, which, together with existence, comes from the ontological differentiation of the *Wesen* precisely in the form of grounding and existence. Inasmuch as it is *the source of the primitive movement* of the state of *Indifference*, *Un-grund* is not resolved once and for all in the ontological distinction and in the subsequent reconciliation thanks to *love*. It remains as a residue, as an unresolved (and unresolvable) excess, always capable of reactivating the process thanks to the *Urwille* (primal will) which has always been a part of it ('*Wollen ist Ursein*'). If it is true – as Heidegger says – that will is divided into biological will and intellectual will,[8] then it does not mean that it can be reduced to this scission: rather it remains as the inexhaustible 'ontological-dynamic reserve' of Being, that is as the 'incomprehensible basis of reality in things, the irreducible remainder (*der nie aufgehende Rest*), which cannot be resolved into reason by the greatest exertion' and that 'unruly lies ever in depths as though it might break out again'.[9]

The *excess* of Reality, which institutes and founds the process of the becoming of Being, is described by Schelling as Pure Will and, similarly, Nietzsche defines this alogical space, which presides over the form of the existent, as Will to Power in its *Dionysian* sense: expressions that are simply meant to make 'humanly comprehensible' a sphere that cannot be thought, which maintains within itself a *dynamics* capable of passing from pure Being, absolutely placed, compact and impenetrable (blind), to the singular determinations of the existent, possible thanks to that coming together of Being which shows, in the fracturing of Being itself (*Seinsfuge*), the possibility of *being in potency* and therefore the existence of the beings (*Seienden*). In this ontological itinerary, it is useful to trace the evolution of Schelling's concept of *Un-grund*, which we will see act, within the thinking of the Leonberg-born philosopher, as a link between Being as 'identity of the identity and of difference' and the *unvordenkliches Seyn* of positive philosophy,[10] where it will be definitively clarified, in Aristotelian terms, as *purely contingent*.

Heidegger's need to differentiate Being as *Ereignis* from Schelling's Absolute[11] was, after all, dictated by the incurable theoretical affinity that essentially thrusts its roots into the *over-realism* that links Heidegger and Schelling (and obviously, I believe, Friedrich Nietzsche) in the conclusive phases of their respective philosophical paths and which, in trying to consider Being (and the 'truth of Being') beyond the existent, inevitably concentrates on the *ontological-dynamic* development and on the original 'giving of self' of the forms of the existent. In actual fact, the impossibility of conceptually dealing with the Beginning, the indomitable initial excess from which every possible form of Being (inasmuch as it is present) historically (*seynsgeschichtlich*) derives, leads Heidegger to consider Being as *Ereignis*. Since Heidegger cannot qualify the 'giving of self' of the event itself as *energheia*, or as *actualitas* – to use terms that are appropriate to metaphysical thinking, according to Heidegger, who, while he believes he is speaking of the Being, is in fact still speaking of the beings – and since he cannot trace a Subject (the *Es* of *Es gibt*) that *gives* the forms in which it presents itself,[12] Heidegger turns to the 'giving', thus attempting the theoretical path of Being as *Ereignis*. In this sense, confronting the consideration of Schelling's Absolute, Heidegger insists on the differences between the ontological nature of *Ereignis*, arguing that the Absolute is the 'matter (*Sache*) itself' inasmuch as it is unconditional subjectivity, conceived, in its essential nature, as 'voluntary reason', and that it is precisely here that the motility of the Absolute itself lies, which only apparently coincides with that which the 'concept of the history of Being thinks of as *Ereignis*'. Nevertheless, Heidegger states:

> Being itself is experienced in *Ereignis* as Being, not as a being and not at all posited as the unconditional being and the highest being, although Being presences, after all, as that which alone 'is'. The Absolute, on the contrary, is what it is in terms of the *abandonment of Being* of beings like every 'being', yes, even more essentially than every being, only that precisely in the subjectivity of the Absolute the abandonment of Being is most of all hidden and cannot appear.
>
> The 'Absolute' is beings as a whole in such a way that knowledge of beings as a whole, and as such knowledge which knows itself to be such, constitutes the 'Being' of beings. Beings 'are' there as this knowledge and 'are' beings in the 'element' of the (unconditional) concept.[13]

In the interpretation presented by Heidegger, Schelling's Absolute is to be seen as a Being among others, or rather as the unconditional entity which, in absolute subjectivity (*Urständlichkeit*), reveals in an even more essential manner (with respect to the other entities) the abandonment of Being in favour of the beings. This description of Schelling's Absolute responds, however, to a somewhat simplified scheme that reduces it to the subjectivity of a supreme Being, that knows itself (and so the being as a whole) through its '*voluntary* reason'. The development of the idea of an Absolute, which matures in Schelling halfway between the conclusions of his philosophy of the Identity (I am thinking particularly of the *System der gesamten Philosophie* of 1804) and the considerations of freedom in *Philosophical Investigations*, leads to the distinction of the Essence in *Wesen* inasmuch as it is existent and in *Wesen* inasmuch as it is grounding, on the basis of an original *Indifference*: an *Un-grund* (non-grounding) that identifies itself as 'Absolute *par excellence*'. This must not be seen as the sudden (though delayed, with respect to the formulation of the concept of Identity strongly opposed by Hegel) introduction by Schelling of an expedient that could save the overall validity of his discourse. In actual fact, already in the writings from the period of the philosophy of Identity, there was a clear ontological distinction between the Absolute *par excellence* (that as such can never be objectively present and always abstains in a *urständliches* X that 'gives' *Sein* to the beings) and its propositions, manifestations: forms, potency of the Absolute. For Schelling, in fact, every being lives a double life: one in the infiniteness of the Absolute and the other in its finitude. The essential difference lies precisely in the fact that the 'doctrine of the potencies' (*Potenzenlehre*) which was meant to describe the 'manifestation' or the dynamic development of the Absolute, including its self-knowledge, did not concern the *Absolute as such* but always, still, highlighted an *excess* that could never be totally resolved in the dynamic proposed, nor even in a conceptual synthesis. The absolute subjectivity (as *Urständlichkeit*) of which Heidegger speaks is not in fact to be seen as the position of a Subject empowered to the point where it coincides with the Object; in Schelling, the Absolute (or the absolute subjectivity) is instead the *Urständlichkeit* that can never be understood objectively, or rather can never be construed as an object of the thought. It remains an absolute position from which, however, the movement of the totality of the beings and the forms of Being (inasmuch as they can be described through a 'doctrine of potencies'[14]) do not proceed simply in a conceptual manner. It is therefore evident that it is not possible to think of Schelling's Absolute as the *concealment* of the *abandonment of Being in favour of the beings*: Schelling's Absolute as such offers (inasmuch as it is *potentia potentiae*) the forms of Being in which the Absolute itself is manifested, but it always remains beyond them as an inexhaustible *residue* always capable of regenerating, so to speak, *seynsgeschichtlich*, the movement of Being and its *dynamic*.

In his attempt to mark the distance of Being as *Ereignis* from Schelling's Absolute, Heidegger then adds, if only briefly, a particularly significant consideration that is worth looking into. Again, in the seminar notes from 1941 to 1943, he writes that 'the Absolute is the Being in its totality (*das Seiende im Ganzen*) so that the knowledge of this entity in its totality constitutes the essence of the entity'. Such a statement is possible only in the binding conviction according to which the Absolute is the existent in its totality, or the totality of that which it is inasmuch as it is objectively present. As I have already said, however, such a presumed totality could not include the residual sphere which, on the one hand, resists the translation of the beings as objectively present and, on the other hand, guarantees its constant renewal. Heidegger then adds that the knowledge (*Wissen*) of this Being in its totality precisely constitutes the essence of the Being, since this knowledge naturally coincides with the motility of the Absolute inasmuch as it is the Absolute's *will* to know itself. From this point of view there is no gap and everything is resolved in a closed Becoming, commanded by a *will* that translates everything into *knowledge*: 'The entity "is" as this knowledge, and "is" existing in the "element" of the (unconditional) concept.'[15]

According to this statement, knowledge, from Schelling's perspective, would assume the total character of *logical science* and the System of knowledge can be traced to the unconditional Concept and its movement. However, this is exactly what Schelling perceives as impossible from the very first stages of his philosophy of Nature and, particularly, in consideration of the apparently asystematic results of *Philosophical Investigations*, which would instead lead him to reconsider, first of all through his attempted *Weltalter-project*, the possibility of a System of philosophy as a dynamic System, and, subsequently, to set out the distinction between negative philosophy and positive philosophy. Moreover, in the reading of the Absolute suggested by Heidegger, the central aspect of Schelling's philosophy from the time of the essay *Über die Möglichkeit einer Form der Philosophie überhaupt* ('On the Possibility of a Form of Philosophy in General') published in 1794, is neglected. This is the identification of a principle of knowledge from which it is possible to 'deduce' (*ab-leiten*) the forms of Being: a principle that Schelling progressively realizes he must identify in what *exceeds* the sphere apparently dealt with by Kantian categories[16] (acquisitions that Schelling considers valid, but which require a principle that justifies them and leads them to the System). Schelling's Absolute must therefore certainly be perceived as the existent in its totality, but in an essential unit with a (free and dynamic) principle that overcomes the Being of the existent inasmuch as it is knowledge and it appears precisely as a non-deducible Principle of the becoming of Being. The progress of *Andere Deduktion der Principien der positiven Philosophie* (*Another Deduction of the Principles of Positive Philosophy*), written in 1839 (and to which we will return in order to show the points of contact with Heidegger's thought of Being as *Ereignis*), also lies in this same tension, in which it is again emphasized that the true task of Schelling's philosophy is after all 'to find [...] the true Monad, that is what is permanent, the principle that stands above all things'. In these terms it would seem we are dealing with a metaphysical principle in the sense expressed by Heidegger, that is a form of onto-theology that perceives Being as starting from a grounding and with the language typical of a certain 'history of being'. In truth, and we will see this in the specific, in this brief essay Schelling moves with great care over the terrain of the ultimate principle, in continuity with the concept of *Un-grund*, cautiously avoiding formulations of a metaphysical kind; and it is precisely in this tension, which we could call *post-metaphysical*, that it is possible to grasp the affinity – Heidegger himself notes it, although as a danger, rather than as a resource – with Being as *Ereignis* that comes as an epilogue to 'the history of being'.

2 Thinking of the positive

In actual fact, the definition of *Ereignis* is somewhat problematic and directly involves Heidegger's entire ontological conception. Although Heidegger, in a particular phase of his thought in which he dedicates great attention to the question of *technique*, perceives the world as 'total organisation/im-position'

(*Gestell*) as 'a first urgent spark of *Ereignis*', this later certainly cannot be reduced to the world as *Technik*, as the phenomenon that describes the unfolding and the achievement of metaphysics:

> What it indicates happens only in the singular [in the system as *Gestell*], no, not in any number, but uniquely. What we experience in the frame as the constellation of Being and man through the modern world of technology is a prelude to what is called the event of appropriation (*Ereignis*). However this latter does not necessarily linger on its prelude, since in the event/appropriation it announces the possibility that it overcomes the mere dominion of the system in a more initial happening (Beginning).[17]

I think that the very meaning of *Ereignis* – as a new beginning – can be traced back to his *Contributions to Philosophy*,[18] where Heidegger begins to think of it as the keyword in his philosophy of the 'turn' after *Being and Time*, as he affirms in his *Letter on Humanis*. Here we find some characterizations and descriptions of the concept of *Ereignis* which could be compared with the particular notion of Schelling's Absolute, as will become even more plausible during the 1962 conference *On Time and Being*. Before describing the content of this intense and illuminating conference, it is necessary to highlight some crucial passages from *Contributions to Philosophy*, written – as we know, between 1936 and 1938 – in a period during which the works of Schelling and Nietzsche were certainly at the centre of Heidegger's thought.

To understand the description of the *Ereignis* offered by Heidegger in this complex work, which remained unpublished until 1989, it is necessary to go back to the meaning and importance within his thought of the 'turn' made after *Being and Time*. In the first instance, the reversal contained within the 'turn' is summed up in the passage from the search for the 'meaning of being' in *Being and Time* to the thought of the 'truth of being' in the years immediately following the writing of his masterpiece, which remained incomplete. This reversal remains in any case intrinsically linked to the *Dasein*. If already in *Being and Time*, being-there (*Dasein*) could no longer be understood as a subject that represents the entity as its 'object', but as a 'projection' (*Entwurf*) that includes the 'meaning of being', then in the years of the 'turn' Heidegger claimed that this could not in any way mean that being is reduced to the 'projection' of being-there, since it is the being-there that is above of all 'thrown' (*geworfen*) from Being itself. From this point of view, being-there certainly remains fundamental, but it becomes a place for the openness of the 'truth of being', or rather of the *Lichtung* of Being, which is precisely the place where freedom happens. In fact, when Heidegger clarifies the meaning of the 'turn' after *Being and Time*, he explicitly refers to the theses contained in the 1930 conference on the *Essence of Truth*, published however in the 1940s: here Heidegger shows how being and thought both belong in the unique event (*Ereignis*) of their happening, and specifies in a rather enlightening way how 'the essence of truth is clarified as freedom', in continuity – we could observe – with the theses of Schelling's *Philosophical Investigations*. Placing the essence of truth within freedom does not mean assigning it to man as his will, because freedom is not to be understood as an *Eigenschaft* (asset in terms of faculty) of man, because it is rather man who is the *Eigentum* (asset in terms of possession) of freedom. 'Freedom', Heidegger writes, 'is the grounding of the intrinsic conformity [of the assertion of truth, or of the thought of being]. [...] Freedom now turns out to be the letting-be of entity', which is to be understood as 'letting oneself be involved with the entity', that is, with that which is open in its openness or, to use the expression used by Heidegger in the first edition (1943), as 'leaving to that which is present (*dem Anwesende*) its presencing (*Anwesen*)'.[19] In this sense, therefore, freedom, even before freedom for action and decision, even before negative or positive freedom, is to be understood as 'letting oneself be involved in the unconcealment of the entity as entity, [and the unconcealment], in turn, is preserved in the letting oneself be involved with the existent, thanks to which the openness of the open, that is, the 'there' [*Da*] of the being-there is what it is'.[20] This freedom is directly linked with Schelling's *Un-grund* of *Philosophical Investigations* and with its original and permanent dynamic, that is with that grounding/non-grounding that Schelling describes both as Indifference and as *schlechtin betrachtet* (absolutely considered) Absolute.

Moreover, within *Ereignis* as event-appropriation is also the *Enteignis*, that is, the ex-propriation: in fact, the essence of truth coincides not only with the manifestation of entities but also with the manifestation of what is hidden, of what is not revealed, that is, with the manifestation of what remains veiled as excess – a concept that, if we wish, has much to do with the 'irreducible remainder' that in Schelling's *Philosophical Investigations* is that grounding (*Grund*) that is based precisely on the groundlessness of the *Un-grund*.

In the progressive approach to the 'definition' of *Ereignis* that he tries to trace in his *Contributions to Philosophy*, Heidegger greatly aligns himself – more or less consciously, that is not important – with the attempts at grounding that are typical of Schelling's positive philosophy, understood as the attempt to think of being from within, in its free and unfounded becoming. The various attempts at grounding in Schelling's philosophy bear witness to the fact that the philosopher's true purpose was to lay the foundations for a 'new' thought, in constant action, that would welcome the Being in its original and permanent creation-grounding and that would continue creation itself.

If, as we saw in the previous chapter, Löwith can advance the hypothesis that the 'facticity' of the existential analytic of *Being and Time* seemed to take its cue from the *existentia* of Schelling's positive philosophy, then it is precisely in the notion of the *Wirklichkeit* that lies at the basis of the aforementioned *Dass* of the existent that the freedom and abyssality of Being – which the Heidegger of the 'turn' directly deals with – is enclosed. On the other hand, Heidegger is very explicit about the concept of *existentia* in the lecture on the *Essence of Truth*.

> The essential grounding of man is concealed in the being-there, that grounding which, for a long time unfounded, allows man to e-xist. Here 'existence' does not mean *existentia* in the sense of occurring or being at hand [*Vorhandensein*]. Nor on the other hand does it mean, in an 'existentiell' fashion, the moral endeavour of the human being on behalf of his 'self' [...]. The Ek-sistence, rooted in truth as freedom, is exposure to the disclosedness of being as such [...]. The existence of historical human

beings begins at the moment when the first thinker takes a questioning stand with regard to the unconcealment of beings by asking: what are beings?. In this question unconcealment is experienced for the first time. Beings as a whole reveal themselves as *physis*, 'nature', which here does not yet mean a particular sphere of beings but rather being as such as a whole, specially in the sense of upsurgent.[21]

From this passage one can observe how Heidegger's 'turn' is fulfilled precisely in the direction of a positive philosophy that is rooted in the freedom and becoming of the Being itself, understood as a free *Physis* that emerges to the entities inasmuch as they are present and remains as an inexhausted grounding for the emergence of ever new happenings of being: in this sense, *Ereignis* describes the temporal happening of this continuous and permanent (*bleibende*) emerging that is the Being itself. The use of the expression 'nature' to refer to the freedom of the entity in its totality is not trivial, nor should it be neglected in any way, as we will see later. It is an extraordinary echo, in my opinion, of Schelling's positive philosophy and his attempts at grounding, which are attributable to the results of his positive philosophy.[22]

Another point of contact with positive philosophy concerns the argumentative style. For the analysis of the unfounded grounding of being, Schelling can only refer to a speculative thought: the privileged object of positive philosophy is first and foremost and for the most part the 'grounding' of being itself, or rather the deduction of the principles of the existent, and since one cannot make use of a mechanical and necessary thought.[23] In order to think about the freedom of the existent in its original grounding, it is necessary to refer to a free thought that is speculative. Heidegger moves in a similar way in his *Contributions to Philosophy* which, by his own admission in the epigraph at the beginning of the text, is only an outline yet to be developed.[24]

> This thinking-saying is a *directive*. It indicates the free sheltering of the truth of Being in beings as a necessity, without being a command. Such a

thinking never lets itself become a doctrine and withdraws totally from the fortuitousness of common opinion. But such thinking-saying directs the few and their knowing awareness when the task is to retrieve man from the chaos of not-being (*das Unseiende*) into the pliancy of a reserved creating of sites that are set up for the passing of the last god.[25]

In Heidegger's speculative quote, the Being gets ready for its leap towards the 'grounding' of his truth 'as a preparation for the 'ones to come' and for the last god'.[26] For Heidegger the new beginning presupposes a listening and the gamble of a questioning for which few are ready,[27] and the *Ereignis* is therefore delineated as a (speculative) hypothesis which can describe the happening of Being in the clearing (*Lichtung*) that the *Dasein* itself is.

The last God – a figure also present in Schelling – is described in the last of the six *Fugen*[28] of which the work *Contributions to Philosophy* is composed and inspired by Hölderlin's *Götterung* (becoming-God), that is to say by the divine happening, as a possibility of still thinking about the gratuitousness of the giving of Being as a gift from a post-metaphysical and non–onto-theological God, after Nietzsche's 'death of God'.

Another aspect that further confirms the closeness of Heidegger's speculation in these pages to the fundamental theses of Schelling's positive philosophy is the recognition that thought, coessential to the being, has the ability to create and continue being itself, an idea that Schelling took directly from his *Naturphilosophie* where he stated – by an intuition that must necessarily be extended to positive philosophy[29] – that 'thinking about nature means creating nature itself'.[30]

The question of being is the leap into Being which man as seeker of Being enacts, insofar as he is one who creates in thinking. The one who seeks Being, in the ownmost overflow of seeking power, is the poet who 'founds' Being.[31]

Thought is not something applied to being, but rather grows with being itself, increasing and creating it. It is not by chance that Heidegger speaks of a 'turn' of Being that concerns being itself and not simply the way of describing it.

The foregoing has directly to do with the notion of the 'essence of truth' of the homonymous conference, in that it coincides with freedom: what the Metaphysics of German Idealism ends up recognizing, precisely with Schelling's *Philosophical Investigations* – which Heidegger recognizes as the 'summit' (*Gipfel*) of that philosophical programme[32] – is that one cannot avoid recognizing freedom as the necessary (given the premises) 'grounding' of Being, a grounding that at the same time, however, is recognized as 'impossible', since it exceeds the theses of metaphysics that comes to fruition precisely in the identification of freedom with the principle of being in general.

As said, this freedom cannot be understood as the faculty of man but, precisely because man is the property of freedom, Being happens in man as *Dasein*, as *Lichtung*, the openness of Being.

> In and *as Dasein*, Being en-owns (ereignet) the truth which it manifests as the non-granting, as that domain of hinting and withdrawal – of stillness – wherein the arrival and flight of the last god are first determined.[33]

In the thought of the freedom of being, the centrality of the *Dasein* is affirmed as a place in which being happens and in which the *Ereignis* of the co-belonging, of the temporal growing together, of being itself, is realized through thought and language. Here we can see an extraordinary closeness to the Schellingian theme of the *Mitwissenschaft* (co-*scientia*) of creation: the truth and freedom of Being happens and is preserved in man, and man alone is therefore given the possibility of continuing creation, giving rise to new beginnings of Being.

For Heidegger, the event as the other beginning, the new beginning to come, happens in the being-there (*Dasein*). The first beginning thinks Being as presence (*Anwesenheit*), while thinking Being as *Ereignis* prepares another beginning; while the grounding-attunement of the first beginning is deep wonder (*Er-staunen*), the grounding-attunement of the other beginning is deep foreboding (*Er-ahnen*).[34] This prediction is described precisely in the form of a speculative hypothesis in view of a future to come that will be fulfilled in the being-there (*Dasein*) itself. And yet it is not a future that can be fulfilled passively beyond the will of man, it is rather an event to be prepared in the form of the reservedness (*Verhaltenheit*), which is

> The style of inconceptual thinking only because it must become the style of future humanness, one grounded in Dasein, because it thoroughly attunes and carries this grounding [...]. The reservedness is the strongest and at the same time the gentlest preparedness of *Dasein* for en-ownment (*Er-eignis*), for being thrown into the owned standing within the truth of the turning in the *Ereignis*.[35]

If in the age of metaphysics the oblivion of being put it in a position to be able to experience amazement and *wonder* in front of the entity as presence, then in the present age, which prepares for the future of the last god, in the age of expanded nihilism, the forgetfulness of oblivion allows, according to Heidegger, for the possession and management of the entity as our own product. However, *reservedness* (*Verhaltenheit*) is the form that disposes the *Dasein* to welcome the being as *Ereignis*, because as a refusal to the entity, it is understood that within this Echo of the being as a refusal, the abandonment of the being is the same grounding as the forgetfulness of the being.

> A being is (*ist*). Being holds sway (*west*).
> Being (as event, *Ereignis*) needs beings so that Being may hold sway (*wesen*) [...].
> Understood from within the truth of Being, what is an 'actual' being is a not-being (*das Unseiende*) under the domination of what is not ownmost to shine, a shining whose origin therein remains hidden.[36]

Ereignis ereignet – this is what we can say about the event-appropriation, but in the same language that speaks about it, there are the onto-theological risks that must be overcome and that, in my opinion, are well highlighted in the *Time and Being* conference.

I believe in fact that a certain approximation to what Heidegger means by *Ereignis*, in particular since he feels obliged to separate this idea from assimilation with a certain concept of the Absolute (and with the coincidence of the *Gestell* of the *technique*), can be given by the content of the conference *Time and Being* broadcast on the radio on 29 January 1962, and read by Heidegger at the University of Freiburg two days later. One passage from this lecture is quite illuminating with regard to the questions we are considering and the prospect of identifying a possible proximity between *Ereignis* and the Absolute:

> To think Being itself explicitly requires disregarding Being to the extent that it is only grounded and interpreted in terms of beings and for beings as their ground, as in all metaphysics. To think Being explicitly requires us to relinquish Being as the ground of beings in favour of the giving which prevails concealed in unconcealment, that is, in favour of the It gives. As the gift [*Gabe*] of this It gives, Being belongs to giving. As a gift, Being is not expelled from giving. Being, presencing [*Anwesen*] is transmuted. As allowing-to-presence, it belongs to unconcealing; as the gift of unconcealing it is retained in the giving. Being is not. There is, It gives Being as the unconcealing; as the gift of unconcealing it is retained in the giving.[37]

Heidegger insists on the fact that *Ereignis* must not be confused with a way of being, since this would take the concept beyond the confines of metaphysical thinking. We must rather consider *Ereignis* as *making happen*. In this sense, however, Heidegger tends to introduce a certain prudence since, in stating this, he perilously skirts a typically metaphysical sphere.

'The historical nature of the history of Being is determined', states Heidegger, 'only starting from the way in which being happens (*geschieht*), that is the way in which being gives itself'. From this point of view, the 'giving' is described as *sending* (*Schicken*) the Being, in which both the *Who* sends and the *sending* itself abstain in an X that can never be grasped.

In reconstructing the 'history of Being' supplied by Heidegger, Western philosophy neglected the 'It' that *gives* (the *Es* in *Es gibt*) in favour of the *gift* (the being inasmuch as it is a gift) that is given by 'It'.

The technical nub of the lecture we are considering lies in the question that intends to investigate the possibility of identifying the roots of *sending* and the *Who* of this 'action'. It is immediately evident that this can become the central problem only thanks to the essential merging of Being and Time, a problem that already characterized – in what we could call a propaedeutic form – *Sein und Zeit*, although starting from quite different theoretical positions, and how the question can hardly be resolved by the identification of a subject to which the 'responsibility' (clearly a metaphysical concept that directly refers to a ground identifiable on the basis of the principle of sufficient reason) of the intending can be attributed.

> The destiny in which It gives Being lies in the extending of time. Does this reference show time to be the 'It' that gives Being? By no means. For time itself remains the gift of an 'It gives' [*Es gibt*] whose giving preserves the realm in which presence is extended. Thus the 'It' continues to be undetermined, and we ourselves continue to be puzzled.[38]

The enigmatic nature of *Es gibt* (the impersonal form that in German introduces what is objectively present) cannot therefore be clarified by the overlapping with 'Time', almost as if it were the Subject that *gives* the Being; Time is rather constituted together with the Being *in the* same *giving* as *Es gibt*.

In Heidegger's language, which is quite different from the terminology and arguments of the Metaphysics of German Idealism, we find the Schellingian problem of the creation *in* time and of the Beginning as a supra-temporal passage from the infiniteness of the Absolute to the finite determinations of Being.

The solution suggested coincides with the introduction of the *Ereignis*, which, in its rich etymological articulation appears to be capable, in Heidegger's view, on the one hand, of describing a 'relation' that is no longer metaphysical between Being and Time and, on the other, of emphasizing the *destinal* nature of the 'history of Being'.

> In the sending of the destiny of Being, in the extending of time, there becomes manifest a dedication, a delivering over into what is their own, namely of Being as presence and of time as the realm of the open. What determines both, time and Being, in their own, that is, in their belonging together, we shall call: *Ereignis*, the event of Appropriation. *Ereignis* will be translated as Appropriation or event of Appropriation. One should bear in mind, however, that 'event' is not simply an occurrence, but that which makes any occurrence possible.[39]

Nevertheless, in this overlapping, constituted of the *Ereignis* and which essentially characterizes Being and Time, we note the theoretical need to displace, beyond the 'character proper to' Being as presence and Time as the sphere of the open, the aim of the philosophical discourse, which becomes ever more clearly the *giving self* of *Es gibt*: that is the 'authentic' and ultimate potential of the original and permanent Being as Beginning.

> In the expressions '*Es gibt Sein*' and '*Es gibt Zeit*', the *Es* that gives in 'It gives Being', 'It gives time', proves to be Appropriation. The statement is correct and yet also untrue: it conceals the matter at stake from us; for, unawares, we have represented it as some present being, whereas in fact we are trying to think presence as such.[40]

The *Es* can therefore be traced to the *Ereignis*. Nevertheless, this course, formally correct in terms of philosophical language, still moves in the direction of the metaphysical thinking of onto-theo-logy, since the *Ereignis* is perceived as a sort of initial Cause (*Ur-sache*) that determines the forms and fate of Being. After all, not even Schelling's Absolute can be said to 'determine' its forms in a causal chain. The *unprethinkable being* placed at the start of the process cannot in fact be represented as the origin, as the primal cause: in the becoming dynamics described by Schelling in *Another Deduction of the Principles of Positive Philosophy*, we in effect witness the formulation of a thought, that we could also call post-Heideggerian, scrupulously careful not to reason in metaphysical terms (in the Heideggerian sense of the expression) and designed to show, by making use of the resources of Aristotelian thinking on the relationship between the contingency and the necessary, the ultimate possibility of positive philosophy which perceives beings as starting from Being itself.

The *Es* of the *Ereignis* of Heidegger and the *unprethinkable being* of Schelling are to be intended as 'that which, no matter how early we come on the scene, is already there'.[41] Both the *Es* of the *Ereignis* and the *unprethinkable being* are not to be intended as a Principle in the form of a metaphysical cause: their absolute *position* that precedes any possible thoughts about it coincides with their common pure *contingency*. This aspect is to be read in connection with the *Nichts* (Nothingness) as an inexhausted source of being that allows the absolutely free position of dynamical and over-realistic Principles, that can determine every form of Being and can allow the knowledge of them.

4

The positive beyond the presence

1 Being that withdraws from the presence

Ereignis cannot therefore present itself as causation, but rather as free (co-) possibility of being: of *Ereignis* we could say that it *ereignet*. And the *Es* that gives, in its possible and formally correct approach to *Ereignis*, can only be understood if it is traced, within Heidegger's philosophical trail, to the *Nichts* of the 1929 conference *Was ist Metaphysik?*. But to confirm a theoretical path and verify its soundness, it is necessary first to linger, in tracing our steps, on another fundamental moment of Heidegger's philosophy, that is on his *Letter on Humanism* of 1946. In the Heideggerian 'turn', which from Being as presence moves directly to Being, the need for a concept that exceeds the logical-conceptual cage of metaphysical language, in order to take up Being in its original authenticity, is increasingly evident. On this path, it is clear that this sphere escapes the possible ontological determinations and that Heidegger must refer to *Nichts* which reveals to man the *anguish* (as we have seen, a crucial concept in *Sein und Zeit* and traceable – in Schelling's view of the philosophy of Identity – to the misery of the finite that man feels when realizing that he lives a double life in the Absolute), showing himself as 'that which [although hidden in its originality] makes possible the manifestness of the entity as such for the human being'.

The space of this original Being, which is certainly to be connected to Nothingness, is however even more clearly described in the *Letter on Humanism* as the authentically 'potential' place of Being (in the subjective sense of the genitive).

Also in this case, Heidegger's discourse certainly cannot follow the terminology and the argumentative style of German Idealism, yet the concepts, we feel we can say, appear to extraordinarily overlay those of Schelling, since Heidegger attempts to define the conditions of possibility for a thinking that can reason on an original and unprethinkable being.

> Thinking is of being inasmuch as thinking, propriated by being (*ereignet*) belongs to being [...]. Thinking is – this says: Being has embraced its essence in a destinal manner in each case. To embrace a 'thing' or a 'person' in their essence means to love them, to favour them (*sie mögen*). Thought in a more original way, such favouring means the bestowal of their essence as a gift. Such favouring (*Mögen*) is the proper essence of enabling (*Vermögen*) which not only can achieve this or that, but also let something essentially unfold in its provenance (*Herkunft*), that is, let it be [...] This enabling is the proper 'possible' (*das eigentliche 'Möglich'*), whose essence resides in favouring ([in the potency to will] *im Mögen*).[1]

In this passage, which on a superficial reading of *Letter on Humanism* might seem irrelevant and simply instrumental to the definition of *technique* that follows, a little later, as the extreme result of the flight of thought from being (from its element), Heidegger instead describes the 'giving' of *Es gibt*, that he previously mentioned in the *dynamic* terms of *potency to will* and which truly has much in common with the eternal *Mögen* of the erstwhile Schelling. Through a consideration of order that we could call supra-modal which, exceeding 'the logical and the metaphysical', restores a concept of 'possible' that does not fall into the opposition between possibility and reality or the distinction between *actus* and *potential*, Heidegger describes the original being, absolutely placed and unprethinkable, as that authentically 'Possible' which 'allows something to be present' (*west*), or which 'makes it be'.

Reading this passage from Heidegger calls to mind a Schellingian extract that dates from the Berlin period:

> It is therefore possible, as we have seen, that is to say, it is *not contradicted by the nature of the existent*, that power follows Being; in fact, *only the purely Existent can be the capable of being*. The *potentia pura*, the beginning of negative philosophy was even incapable of being power and could not keep itself as such. Only the purely Existent is what can be (*das Mächtige*) the *potentia* and since it cannot be power of the act, it is materially already *potentia potentiae*. That which always has its original Being is precisely that something that wants to or can begin, because it has its Being independently of self, it has its Being first and is certain of it.[2]

The quotation from the *Paulus Nachschrift* in the lectures on the philosophy of Revelation is quite explanatory in relation to what Manfred Frank called Schelling's 'return to Kant'. This is clearly not a 'return' to the Kant of *Kritik*, but rather a resumption of a pre-critical theme relating to the concept of Being inasmuch as position (*absolute Setzung*): a concept already explicitly expressed by the philosopher from Königsberg in the essay 'The Only Possible Argument in Support of a Demonstration of the Existence of God' (*Der einzig mögliche Beweisgrund zu einer Demonstration des Daseins Gottes*) which dates from 1763. Schelling's recourse to a Being which, in any case, precedes this thinking responded to the need to define the sphere of rational philosophy and to guarantee the original space from which every form of being can derive. Nonetheless, and this was already outlined to a certain extent in what I said previously, it is not possible to resolve the question of positive philosophy and of Being[3] which has always preceded any thinking on the matter through the reference – however necessary and absolutely philologically verified – to the so-called return to Kant. In fact, while it is true that this 'return' can to a certain extent be traced to Hölderlin and his concept of Being, which Schelling probably took into consideration immediately following the writing of his essay 'Of the I as a Principle of Philosophy', it is also true that in the use that Schelling could make of the modal inversion (which however would immediately become supra-modal) between *possibility* (*Möglichkeit*) and reality (*Wirklichkeit*), in favour of the latter, a fundamental role was played by, on the one hand, the *dynamic* concept that Schelling undoubtedly assigned to this *Wirklichkeit* (probably traceable, to some extent, to a veiled form of *speculative materialism*, dating from the sources of Swabian pietism in his philosophy of Nature) and, on the other, the resumption of the Aristotelian concept of the *contingency* (with respect to the necessary) for the description of the condition (*Urstand*) of the unprethinkable being (*unvordenkliches Seyn*) placed at the Beginning of Everything: truly a fundamental element of the essential conflict between Freedom and Necessity. We will see further on that the introduction of the *purely* contingent, as the essential nature of the unprethinkable being, can only be confirmed by the passage from this to the 'process', which is possible through the juxtaposition and the tension of *what simply can be* (*das Seynkönnende*), and therefore only as the process (necessarily) activated (only after the 'position' of the *purely* contingent) can the forms and the qualifications of being be defined; and this in a surprising affinity with what Heidegger has to say with respect to the *Ereignis*, or the *Es* of *Es gibt*, which is Nothingness and nevertheless becomes that *Es* (that non-grounding, that *Un-grund*, that unprethinkable being, to use Schelling's terminology), which, as *purely* contingent (original), guarantees the being's capacity for existing. In the passage quoted we read that only the purely Existent *can be* the capable-of-being and this statement must be read attributing – as Schelling more or less explicitly does – a *transitive meaning* to that being which *can be* the *capable-of-being*.

Such a meaning of Being can be reconstructed (1) by tracing the sovramodal inversion that we have described, with Frank, as a 'return to Kant'; (2) by granting to the Schellingian *Wirklichkeit* the effectual dynamic that can be traced to a form of *speculative materialism* never wholly abandoned by Schelling and dating from the philosophy of Nature and its sources (Oetinger and Hahn); (3) by an analysis (also terminological) of the relationship that constitutes the *essential conflict between necessity and freedom*, between the unprethinkable being as *purely contingent* and *what simply can be* that *becomes capable of commanding*. This analysis that must trace the Schellingian stages of the eternal *Mögen*, described in the Erlangen lectures, and verify how, in Schelling's *Spätphilosophie* and, similarly, in Heidegger's later theoretical considerations, there is after all the *original dynamic of an unprethinkable Being* that determines a possible *ontology*, and that it is therefore the becoming that commands the forms of being.[4]

In support of our somewhat daring conclusions, above all with regard to the Heideggerian perspective and its affinity with the later ideas of Schelling, it may be useful to consider what Heidegger wrote, in his *Letter on Humanism*, shortly after the passage we considered earlier:

> Being is the enabling-favouring [*das Vermögend-Mögende*], the 'may be' (*das Mög-liche*). As the element, being is the 'quiet power' [*stille Kraft*: 'tacit force'] of the favouring-en-abling, that is the possible [...]. When I speak of the *stille Kraft des Möglichen* I do not mean the possible of a merely represented *possibilitas*, nor the *potentia* as *essentia* of an *actus* of *existentia*; rather, I mean being itself, which in its favouring presides over thinking, and hence over the essence of humanity and that means over its relation to being [which is to say to thought].[5]

To see, as Heidegger does, the possible as that which *can act* on being and on the concept of being is to shift our attention to the being that flees from the presence and that in its *capability* 'begins' (in the sense of *ereignet*) the being and its forms: this Being *is* (*west*; while the entity *ist*) inasmuch as it is *Ereignis*; it is not, however, I repeat, a way of being; it is rather that which *can* (in its 'tacit force') the perception of being itself and which shows itself only in the dynamic process, in the *gibt* of *Es gibt* (in the giving of it gives), that is when it *happens*; this is where its *unprethinkable* nature and pure original contingent, and therefore unforeseeable nature originate from.

Yet, this 'tacit force' which *can* being also determines its logical-metaphysical happening and therefore also the grammar which is expressed beginning with the copula; in this Heidegger finds great difficulty in arguing about the being that withdraws from the presence since it freely derives from it. Being cannot be reduced to language as the Gadamerian hermeneutic school would wish, although it is determined by the essential dynamic. Therefore, while it is true that language does not describe Being overall, it is also true that in the hermeneutic penetration of language we can see the original and constitutive dynamic of Being.

2 *Un-grund* and *unvordenkliches Seyn*

In Schelling's work, the concept of *Un-grund* certainly acts as the link between the philosophy of Identity and the division in negative and positive philosophy. The *Un-grund* of *Philosophical Investigations*, described as the original Indifference (not to be confused with the quantitative equivalent – *Gleichgültigkeit* – between the spiritual pole and the natural pole, since this is possible only *within* the development of the Identity), is initially introduced by Schelling in order to free the original Identity from the misunderstanding that it – unjustly seen as sameness – is not legitimized to distinguish between the Real and the Ideal in the manifestation of the Absolute. In fact, however, the original Identity should not be seen as sameness, but rather as the dynamic Identity of Identity and Difference. In this acquisition, which dates from the period of the philosophy of Identity, although Schelling already foresaw an ontological priority to be assigned to the natural pole (and this was evident in the writings dating from the late 1890s on the philosophy of Nature[6]), there was no evidence of a residue impenetrable for reason (or rather for the Spirit) placed at the start of the process and never totally consumable. Rather, he foresaw an organic development of the Absolute (*Gesamtorganismus*) which at every turn, in every degree and stage, maintained a certain quantity of Spirit and a certain quantity of Nature, so that the prevalence of one never wholly annulled the other.

The introduction of *Un-grund* served, however, at the same time, to guarantee the first level of ontological difference, so to speak, between the Absolute as such and the manifestations of the same. If in the philosophy of Identity, Schelling stated that the development (described in the 'doctrine of the powers') exclusively concerned the sphere of the manifestation (of the finite), while the Absolute, inasmuch as it is infinite, could not be understood starting from the 'doctrine' of the powers, then the *Un-grund*, as absolute Indifference (original non-distinction), guaranteed the 'description' of an antepredicative Being capable of 'giving rise to' the dynamic development of the Absolute and at the same time refraining from the manifestation: that is, a being that showed itself as such, as antepredicative, absolutely un-differentiated and standing at the Beginning of Everything, only to start from the dynamic process itself which would then show its *purely* contingent nature, instrumental, so to speak, to the free *necessity* of the process itself.

This concept anticipates the concept of the *unvordenkliches Seyn* that Schelling clarified, also in logical-formal terms, by turning to the thinking of Aristotle.

Before we consider the points of contact between the *Un-grund* and the *unvordenkliches Seyn*, I feel it is useful to emphasize their common origin which, in Schelling's philosophy, is rooted in the concept of the absolute Identity, that he describes in *Darstellung meines Systems der Philosophie* (*An Exposition of My System of Philosophy*), written in 1801. In this retrospective view, it is undoubtedly useful to highlight that Schelling's original problem, that is the identification of a Principle for his System, was already evident in all its complexity at the time of the philosophy of Identity: here, in fact, despite Hegel's later criticism of the static nature of Schelling's system, the Principle, that is to say the Start of the differentiation within the Identity, was already presented as a dynamic Principle:

> § 52. The essence of absolute identity, inasmuch as it is the immediate cause of reality [*Realität*], is *force*. This is clear from the concept of force. Since every immediate grounding of reality is in fact called force.[7]

Schelling's statement must be read with the understanding that the absolute Identity is to be seen as the absolute Reality (*Wirklichkeit*) of being, that is to say Being which, inasmuch as it is an absolute position, determines in its (always becoming) dynamics the successive (in ontological, not chronological, order) distinction of the various realities (*Realitäten*), forms, of being. Moreover, it must be observed that Schelling introduces the 'relation' of causality between the Reality of the absolute Identity and the reality of the being; nonetheless, this relation is totally extraneous to the principle of sufficient reason since the adverb 'immediately' excludes a causal chain describable in time and introduces, instead, the concept of 'force' inasmuch as it is inherent in the absolute Identity. In fact, shortly afterwards Schelling adds that 'the absolute Identity as the immediate grounding of the reality of A and B is *force*'. If X is the absolute Identity, then A and B are 'determined' by X inasmuch as it is force or 'immediate grounding of reality'. But not even the verb 'to determine' can clarify the formula that 'imposes' the reality of A and B beginning from the X of the absolute Identity. This formula, as Manfred Frank, better than others, shows, lies in the *transitive* meaning of the copula: X '*is*' (in the *transitive sense*[8]) A and B. In this the original identity of X, which exists in both A and B is preserved, and at the same time we see the internal differentiation of the absolute Identity of X, which in itself (i.e. without differentiation) *is not*, or is equal to Nothingness (οὐκ ὄν).

In our interpretation, nonetheless, we intend to insist on what Schelling places at the origin of being, since we feel that without this thorough investigation we would simply be dealing with a formal aspect of his ontology and not with the essentially conflictual nature that arises from the *dynamic* that lies behind it.

In Schelling's philosophy of Identity, the copula expresses the *force* that 'lets' the reality of being 'be'. For Schelling, therefore, the origin of the distinction is a *force*, or rather, the antepredicative Being of the absolute Identity (which will be later described as *Un-grund* and subsequently as *unvordenkliches Seyn*) cannot avoid containing the *force* that pushes it (in the attraction) towards the Beginning; without it, this would remain in its non-being and its dynamic development would never see the light of day. However, if at the origin of Being, in the non-grounding of the absolute Identity and therefore even before the relation to A and B, a *force* (or a field of forces) is posited, we can clearly see how 'the basis' of Schelling's ontology – starting from the philosophy of Identity – is first of all a *dynamic* and how this determines in its development, the forms and ways of the ontology itself.

The X that precedes A and B cannot be better described than as the absolute Identity without predicates; it contains, however, *in nuce* both A and B inasmuch as the realities that will be determined by their juxtaposition will be determined starting from *primum existens*, that is from the matter as first totality relating to the differentiation of the Identity, as an attractive force (A) and as an expansive force (B).

In the subsequent development of his philosophy, Schelling does not refer explicitly to the concept of 'force' to describe the essence of the absolute Identity, but as we have already seen in the *Wollen* of *Philosophical Investigations*, it can be understood first of all starting from the original concept. Once again, in my opinion, we must read the introduction of the *eternal Mögen* that summarizes the concepts of *power* and *will*, which will show how this interpretation moves towards a *dynamic ontology* and how this can also contribute to the understanding of the Heideggerian perspective or at least its 'application' in the contemporary philosophical debate.

Let us therefore continue bearing in mind that, in our interpretation, Schelling places at the origin of Being without predicates, absolutely placed and preceding any possible thinking of it, a *force* that makes the Beginning possible. This will serve to understand why, according to the theoretical course we are pursuing, the identification of the *Un-grund* and of the *unvordenkliches Seyn* with a supposition of ontological (or worse, simply epistemological) order cannot clarify the subsequent development of the process nor serve Schelling's philosophical perspective. In particular, in considering the *unvordenkliches Seyn*, Schelling introduces an observation on the absolute Freedom of the Beginning, as *Anfang*, which calls directly on the concept of attractive force; an aspect that will be useful when I discuss the passages from *Grundlegung der positiven Philosophie* (*The Foundations of Positive Philosophy*). After describing the three moments (which I will consider in more depth later) in which the 'prototype of every existence' is (1) the *unprethinkable being*, (2) *what simply can be* opposed to it and (3) the free oscillation between the two, Schelling describes the pure Beginning of existence:

> The beginning of every existent [...] is the pure subject *for* being, this subject, inasmuch as it is not yet existent, is only that which it can be, the simple subject for being, but still without being, and therefore to be thought of *as* pure powerfulness, pure power. This is the internal start of every existence – the *in-itium* (*An-fang*), precisely thanks to the fact that it, through its infinite non-*being*, is the attractive power of the equally infinite being, which is therefore the second, and only the second. *Anfangen* (to begin) and *Anziehen* (to attract) are already equivalent concepts in their literal aspect: in the attraction is the beginning.[9]

Although this description of the Beginning concerns the existence of the entities determined by the will of God, it is necessary to emphasize that for Schelling 'the beginning' presupposes in any case, an attraction, a force that holds and makes possible the Beginning: this aspect cannot be ignored in the authentic beginning of the process that places it in the original passage that opposes *what simply can be* to the *unvordenkliches Seyn*, since – as we will see – they exist in a unity which, although only introduced (in an ontological sense) subsequently to the blind being, they conserve within them that 'force' capable of opposing, in the attraction, the power of being.

What is more, this aspect will serve to understand the fact that in Schelling's *Spätphilosophie*, alongside the use of the Aristotelian doctrine of the act and the power, it is always necessary to consider that in the pure act of existence, inasmuch as it is *potentia potentiae*, is always present a *force* that *can* (in the sense of *make possible*) the being of the existent in addition to its predicative formulation, which is also witnessed by the meaning that again in the philosophy of Revelation Schelling attributes to the copula, in an attempt to emphasize the identitary sovra-relation that presides over the substantial unit of the *unprethinkable being* (which is such only because it opposes the *what simply can be*) and *what simply can be* (which *makes possible* the being, inasmuch as it is the will that passes from power to act).

3 The later Schelling and Aristotle

We have seen that from his earliest works Schelling considered the philosopher's duty to be the identification of the Principle that stands above all else. Now, in the grounding of his positive philosophy the *unprethinkable being* is certainly 'before' everything else inasmuch as it is *purely contingent*, but it cannot be configured as the Beginning of Everything, since it, inasmuch as it exists simply as *actu*, does not preserve a dynamic capacity to act as the Principle, but only as the 'essential presupposition' (*Voraussetzung*), which furthermore appears only in this manner *a posteriori* in the process already underway. In fact, if the *unprethinkable being* is to be defined as 'purely' contingent it must be possible to oppose it to something that can be altered, or something 'with regard to which [...] it can behave as something contingent' – according to the Aristotelian definition.[10]

'The existent necessarily only *actu* [...] is the existent necessarily only contingently',[11] since this excludes *what simply can be* as *antecedens* (due to the fact that in its existing inasmuch as it is absolute Reality, it precedes every possibility) but not in the absolute sense. As we have said, the Kantian doctrine of being which Schelling uses in his later speculations is integrated by means of the

Aristotelian perspective and this contributes, on the one hand, to justifying the logic of *Philosophical Empiricism* and, on the other, to confirming the dynamic perspective that Schelling finds he must definitively introduce with the question of the (ontological) Freedom of the Beginning. Schelling therefore avails himself of the Aristotelian doctrine of the power and the act, in effect overturning it and integrating it through the introduction of the concept of the *purely* contingent. After having emphasized how the true merit of Aristotelian philosophy lies in the profound bond that it establishes with the thought and the being, so that even the *a priori* (field of negative philosophy) is not, as it was with Hegel, 'something empty, a logical thinking that again has as its content only thinking'.[12] In Aristotle, logic, in its effective thinking, speaks to power, but this is only inasmuch as it is led to 'leap into being', that is to pierce the act of existence. In this sense, the *a priori* knowledge speaks directly to that which pierces the being and therefore presents itself as empirical knowledge. Moreover, this is in effect the course taken by Aristotle, just as his doctrine makes possible the passage from the logical to the empirical, so it creates a path from the empirical to the logical, that is to say a way to reach the *logica*, which for Aristotle is 'innate and inherent in nature'.

Schelling traces the Aristotelian doctrine in an attempt to show that even Aristotle at the height of his empirical philosophy reached the ultimate outcome of negative philosophy, colliding with that limit. Starting from the potency which for him corresponds to the beginning, Aristotle comes to the act, in which the oppositions, which are still enveloped in potency, are resolved into pure entelechy, 'out of the womb of indeterminacy and infinitude of potency, of what is possible, nature elevates itself step by step towards its end from which it is attracted'.[13] At the culmination of this gradual progress from potency to the act, Aristotle places God as the End, that which actually exists (*das wirklich Existierende*). As such, however, that which actually exists is not a member of the series, but it is what it is above and independent of the entire series:

> Aristotle has this as that which actually exists (not merely as an idea as in negative philosophy) – and here lies the distinction – but he employs this as

that which actually exists as the final *telos* only because it grounds his entire science in experience.[14]

Although Aristotle considers the world, the object of his rational philosophy, as existing, he still does not possess the existence, since this has a merely *contingent* nature in his philosophy. According to Schelling, since for Aristotle the true purpose of thinking is the essence of things, their what-is, existence is welcomed as a simple presupposition. Consequently, the End, that which actually exists, as pure act, is the End of rational philosophy and Aristotle cannot make use of it, which in fact qualifies it as the ultimate end, as the prime mover, which is the cause of the movement, but it does not pass through an impulse or an action, but rather through a desire that the inferior natures feel towards that which is higher.

> Aristotle so insists that the End is act that God, for him, [...] is no longer mere potency of thought. For him, God is the pure incessant *actus* of thinking (but of no thought without content). As it is difficult for him to say what God is thinking [...], he decides on this basis that God perpetually thinks only himself.[15]

But a 'God' thus described cannot be used by Schelling as an absolutely free creator, dispenser of being; he therefore avails himself of the definitions of the Aristotelian doctrine, in effect distorting them: that is to say, beginning from the 'God' that is not described as pure potency nor simply as act, but rather as a dynamic articulation that has as presupposition the *actus purus* of the *unprethinkable being*, which can nevertheless be described as such only if *what can be (das Seinkönnende)* is opposed to it. According to Schelling, this opposition is, however, possible only thanks to an *essential unity* with the *unprethinkable being*.

In this idea, which Schelling takes up step by step in *Another Deduction of the Principles of Positive Philosophy*, the *purely contingent* nature of what exists is preserved, in fact it is taken up as an inevitable presupposition that is never described as *necessary nature* (this is – as Schelling emphasizes – the error that Spinoza continues to make with regard to his Substance), although it is like the *purely contingent* and as such finally guarantees the absolute freedom of the dynamics that develops: a truly original freedom that still precedes the divine freedom and which coincides with the pure and original freedom described by Schelling in the *Un-grund* of *Philosophical Investigations* in that Nothingness before God that Schelling, like Heidegger, cannot describe, but which preserves in itself all the potential (*das Mächtige*) of Being. In fact, already in 1927/8, in his preparatory notes for the seminar on the *Philosophical Investigations* Heidegger emphasized that the *Un-grund* was introduced by Schelling as that 'Positive that precedes every contrast'.

> What simply can be as such (*das Seynkönnende*) would have no right to exist; however, once the sheer *actu*, i.e. once the merely contingent necessity *is*, the merely possible may assert its demands just as unprethinkable Being first makes it *possible* that the potency appears.[16]

This means, according to Schelling, that *what can be*, which appears later, with respect to the *unprethinkable being*, is not something different from it, but solely and only 'the same as the merely existent': between the two there must be a unity that Schelling defines as *necessary nature*, which, independently from the *actus* of existing, is 'that which necessarily exists in its nature and in its essence'. The true Principle that Schelling's philosophical research seeks is therefore this *necessary nature* which is made up of a 'becoming' organized in three fundamental moments whose *ontological* relationship is only described starting from its original and permanent *dynamics*. While Schelling can distinguish in it: (1) *the unprethinkable being*, insofar as it is purely *contingent*; (2) *what simply can be* other as *necessary* opposition; (3) the *free* fluctuation, insofar as it is pure spirit, between one and the other, he can only do so starting from a *dynamics already underway*, since otherwise it would not make sense to speak of a juxtaposition between that which is *contingent* (the *unprethinkable being*) and that which is 'freely' *necessary* (*what simply can be*). On the basis of this dynamic organization, Schelling therefore tries to construct a postmetaphysical Principle: a *free grounding of Being* that preserves in its permanent dynamics the being in its complexity.

> The *necessary nature* is free 1) towards this other being [different from its unprethinkable being]; free, that is, a) to not want it: in fact, also independently from this being and before it, it is (it exists) and it is *a priori* certain of this. But also free b) to want this being, having precisely in the *actus* of the unprethinkable existing that which makes it possible to be also lord of that other being [...].
>
> The *necessary nature* would also be equally free [...], 2) from the unprethinkable being itself: it is not forced to persist in it, but can leave it behind, it can make of this immemorial being itself once again a pure moment of its movement, of its life.[17]

The freedom referred to here is therefore merely ontological as witnessed above all by its relation to the preference for existence that is rooted (as already shown in *Philosophical Investigations*) in the eternity: when the Possibility (what simply can be) unexpectedly encounters Reality (the unprethinkable being), that thus *is* (exists). This *unprethinkable being* takes on a negation, a power, thus becoming an existent: 'it does not cease to be, in its essence, in the state of *actus purus*, but it is no longer *actu*, but rather only essence, and, since essence is = power, it is therefore now only the infinite power of the *actus purus*'.[18] From the *purely contingent* being that it was it has now become capable of posing or not posing this contingent being, and it has therefore become master of its own original being.

> The necessarily existent *natura sua* must transcend the existent necessarily only *actu*, it must overtake it, it must be *more* than this. But since in this *more* there cannot again be the existent, because it is already there, it can only be the power of being, and that is the power of being beyond itself, in addition to its own immemorial being. It will not be *potential actus*, since this (*actus*) is already *a priori*, therefore it will only be *potentia potentiae*.[19]

We are therefore already placed on this side of the Principle, which nevertheless can begin to be such only thanks to an unprethinkable being that Schelling adopts only as *purely contingent*, which, being so, requires a 'necessary' (this is how it describes itself *a posteriori*) opposition: the true substantial disagreement, the true essential conflict lies precisely in this original 'determination' (or proto-determination) of being: here the logically irremediable Conflict between the *necessity* and the *freedom* emerges.

But it is time to clarify this aspect: the original, ontological Freedom cannot be that which is contrasted with necessity, since this opposition already occurs in the sphere of that which it is beginning from the dynamic development of the Principle in its three moments (unprethinkable being, what simply can be, free oscillation between the former and the latter); the *ontological, essential and original Freedom, is the Conflict itself that precedes the aforementioned opposition*: that is, it is that indelible and unpronounceable conflict that lies in the *unprethinkable being* (in the Nothingness of the Beginning) and which is described by Schelling in its *pure* contingency, which is contrasted 'with necessity' (at the risk of the persistence of the abyssal Nothingness – of the X that *is not in a transitive sense* A and B – and therefore the impossibility of the reality of the process) to *what simply can be*.

We have seen that the dynamics briefly mentioned described a unity that Schelling also calls – referring to the principles of his philosophy of Identity – *substantial Identity*,[20] meaning that 'precisely this substance, in its unity, and therefore without becoming two, is the potency to be and the purely existent'. We know, moreover, that also in Schelling's later works, the 'force' which constitutes the potency to be, that is the force that makes possible the passage from the potency to the act, is 'pure will'; we are also aware of the fact that for Schelling's philosophy of Identity referred to here, the essence of the absolute Identity, inasmuch as it causes reality (i.e. it brings about that which is inasmuch as it exists), is *force*. But what then will be the 'force' that (necessarily) opposes the *unprethinkable being* (inasmuch as *purely* contingent) to what simply can be in this *substantial identity*? The purely existent can be determined – observes Schelling – as the purely and simply willing, without will, so to speak, as willing that is not preceded by will:

> The simply and infinitely willing [...] is *mere* act, and therefore not even this pierces the power of the act and if we feel and we recognise current reality in general only where such a piercing takes place, then the potency to be and the purely existent constitute a wholly equal *superreality* and, thanks to this wholly equal purity, one does not exclude the other.[21]

As Schelling himself clarifies, he uses the term 'purity' to describe that sphere devoid of the interpenetration of power and act that marks every being inasmuch as it is; in the superreality of this *substantial and original Identity*, even in their 'identity', power and act *are* in their *purity*. Nonetheless, what we mean to clarify is which 'force' actually allows the opposition of the *potency to be* to the *purely existent* and thus gives life to the reality of being:

> The *purely* willing is as Nothingness, precisely because it does not take care of itself, it does not assert itself; but also that which is simply capable of *willing* itself is as Nothingness because it does not really will. The *purely* existent is, precisely because it is such, that which has no power over being [...]. The *purely* existent cannot become, by itself, non-act. For this to occur an opposition is necessary.
>
> But even if the purely existent behaves as that which on its own is incapable of being, then it should not be differentiated from the mere *potency to be*, because the mere *potency to be* is like the *potency not to be*. If, therefore, the power of being is the *same* as the purely existent, then they are not mutually exclusive, but one and the other are the same thing in substantial identity. We have twofold unity.[22]

If then this unity occurs inasmuch as it is *substantial identity* and if between the *potency to be* and the *purely existent* (*unvordenklich*) there is this supra-relation, then the same force that acts in the power of the act (that is will) originally determines the need for the opposition to the unprethinkable being, except that this primordial will (as *Urwille*) remains here suspended between non-will and will: undecided in the essential Conflict that constitutes the ontological Freedom. This *substantially identitary* nature that links the *unprethinkable being* and *what simply can be* also helps us to clarify, taking a step backwards, the nature of the *Un-grund* of *Philosophical Investigations*, which, inasmuch as it is absolute Indifference (absolute and original identity) maintains within it as a compressed Conflict the 'force' destined to show being as essence (*Wesen*) inasmuch as it exists and as essence inasmuch as it is grounding.

Thus we understand how it is not possible to perceive the *Un-grund* nor the *unvordenkliches Seyn* as an empty space lacking force, since this would mean betraying the overall formulation presented by Schelling in the form of a philosophy of absolute (dynamic) Identity which perceives the original contrast on the basis of a (coessential) 'force' posited as the essence itself of the absolute Identity and not as the specific nature of one of the terms constituting the relation. The *superreality* of the substantial identity, therefore, is guaranteed by the force (described as *Urwille*) which activates the dynamic process and which constitutes its essence: without any *force* (that Schelling, as we know, describes as 'will' in order to make it 'comprehensible to human beings') placed at the heart of the *substantial identity*, in the essence of the identitary supra-relation, there would not be that superreality that guarantees and makes possible the various forms of being: that essential tension, that is the conflictual *dynamic* (free *par excellence*) that guarantees Schelling's *ontology*.

It is therefore a dynamic becoming that makes possible the first and original ontological determinations of positive philosophy: the absolutely contingent being of the *unvordenkliches Seyn* and *what simply can be* (*das Seynkönnende*) opposed to it in the conflictual tension. In order to attempt to further deal with this very subtle (and crucial) passage in Schelling's thinking, it is necessary to bear in mind Aristotle's statement regarding the 'contingent' in book VI of *Metaphysics*, since it is precisely starting with such a concept that Schelling attempts to show the *Übergang* or transition from negative philosophy to positive philosophy, the ecstatic about-turn that reason must make in order to see the Existent as such.

> Reason, posited outside itself, for the purpose of negative philosophy, and registered so to speak – since it sees that in this philosophy it cannot possess its *true* content as real content – decides to start from being before any thought. However, it submits to this being only to immediately rebel against it, and this with the problem of *what* the unprethinkably existent is: in this, in fact, reason has first of all and immediately only the unprethinkable existence itself; just as in that deduction from which no-one, as Kant says, can *defend* themselves: 'If something exists (the conditional nature, or assumptiveness, of the expression indicates that here the presupposition is that that which *is* can equally *not be*, therefore *being* is purely accidental), there must exist a *something* (*exactly what* it is remains vague) in a necessary way'.[23]

The introduction of the 'assumptiveness' of the absolute position is due to the fact that reason cannot presume this existence, since this would suppose a grounding for this existence, or a power that passed from the act to existence. But the *unprethinkable being* has nothing that precedes it and therefore has to be described as *purely contingent*, and this alludes directly to the Nothingness of the Beginning.

In fact, Schelling turns to the *contingent* due to the theoretical proximity that occurs between this and being inasmuch as existing as impossible object of reason. No speculation – we read in *Metaphysics* – has the *contingent* as an object. Since Aristotle identifies as a possible object of science that which persists 'always in the same way and due to necessity', not in the sense of constriction, but rather in the sense of that necessity which Aristotle identifies as 'not capable of being in a different way', the contingent, inasmuch as it 'necessarily [is], neither always, nor generally', is not produced by any determined power and therefore is not the subject of science. *The cause of that which is contingent is in turn contingent.*

Therefore, since not all things either are or come to be of necessity and always, but, the majority of things are for the most part, the accidental must exist; for instance a pale man is not always nor for the most part musical, but since this sometimes happens, it must be accidental (if not, everything will be of necessity). The matter, therefore, which is capable of being otherwise than as it usually is, must be the cause of the accidental. And we must take as our starting-point the question whether there is nothing that is neither always nor for the most part. Surely this is impossible. There is, then, besides these something which is fortuitous and accidental. But while the usual exists, can nothing be said to be always, or are there eternal things?[24]

The proximity of the 'accidental' or 'contingent' to 'not-being' (μη όν)[25] certainly explains why Schelling wants to use this concept to describe the being that always comes before the thinking and its coessential original Freedom: moreover, it is through this theoretical theme that Luigi Pareyson's reading traces the Freedom of the Beginning in its inevitable link to Nothingness, suggesting likewise (and we will see how) a reading of the theoretical affinity between Schelling and Heidegger starting with the description that the latter offers on *Nichts* in the conference held in 1929, *Was ist Metaphysik?*.

Nevertheless, this Aristotelian concept allows us to further integrate our overall consideration of *unvordenkliches Seyn*, first of all because we can see that it is 'realised' by the necessity that there should be 'cases' that do not fall within the 'always and generally' – a necessity that perfectly agrees with the fundamental idea of the Schellingian system, which emerges in all its strength in *Philosophical Investigations*, that 'nowhere do we find that the order and the form [are] the original condition, but everywhere things appear as if an original condition without rules has been led towards order'; and, secondly, it is an aspect which must in effect be treated with extreme caution, because it allows us to glimpse *matter* behind this contingent. Aristotle writes that 'the matter, [...] which is capable of being otherwise than as it usually is, must be the cause of the accidentale' (or contingent), but we must remember that Schelling describes the *unvordenkliches Seyn* not simply as contingent but as *purely* contingent, thus emphasizing the impossibility of tracing its grounding to some cause. Yet the Aristotelian passage we mentioned previously, provokingly interrogates us, since we know, and we have extensively discussed, the fact that in Schelling there is a form of *speculative materialism* that dates from the time of the philosophy of Nature, and we also know that this aspect of his speculation is never abandoned in the course of his thinking (take, for example, the theories of Philosophie der Offenbarung (philosophy of Revelation)).

In Schelling's 'overrealism', in the original dynamic that through the opposition of *what simply can be* to the *unvordenkliches Seyn* sets off the ontological process, we have already considered as an intimate essence of this substantial (and dynamic) Identity a 'force' that allows the tension and the process that follows; it cannot therefore be excluded that this force could be that *pure matter*, that 'absolute cause' (to which it is subject in eternity and therefore exceeds the confines of the principle of sufficient reason), that brings about the *purely* contingent of the *unvordenkliches Seyn*: but we are clearly on the plane of pure speculation,[26] and only in this sense are we authorized to formulate this type of hypothesis. Nonetheless, Schelling's introduction to the contingent in the field of positive philosophy, which does not present a formal dialectic but rather the current dialectic in the field of freedom, deals directly with the *material* power of being: 'this contingency posits the possibility of a power that removes [aufhebende] that unprethinkable being [...] The blind being is, due to its contingency, precisely the (material) power of that potency opposed to it.'[27]

The same 'force' that places and maintains in tension the *unprethinkable being* and *what simply can be* (that which can be described as Un-Wille[28] or Urwille) is the 'force' that determines the being in its expressions and in its 'grammar'. From there the *transitive* meaning of the copula which, *being able and wanting to do, commands* being in its various forms: this command is described by Schelling using the expression that we have come across more than once, in particular in the Erlangen lectures of 1821 (Initia philosophiae universae), which is the *Mögen*, an expression by which the meaning of potency (Können) and will (Wollen) are summarized and preserved together.

5

Being that can (make happen) Being

1 The *Abgrund* of Nothingness

Before delving into the analysis of this concept that is decisive for my overall discourse, we must first consider further the relationship between Nothingness and original Freedom in Schelling and on the possible affinity (already verified in other ways) with the last phase of Martin Heidegger's thinking, in particular the concept of being as *Ereignis*. In the essay *Heidegger: la libertà e il nulla* ('Heidegger: Freedom and Nothingness') published in the *Annuario Filosofico* in 1989,[1] Luigi Pareyson, tracing the stages of his approach to Schelling's thinking also through Karl Jaspers's existential thinking, suggests we should read Schelling's Freedom in continuity with the Nothingness of Heidegger's 1929 conference *Was ist Metaphysik?*. In Pareyson's opinion, although Heidegger, given his anti-Christian position, could not genuinely continue Schelling's thinking on Freedom, he arrived at the theory of ontological Freedom by illuminating the essential connection with the Nothingness described in that historical conference. Pareyson's real purpose is to propose, through a theoretical combination, a radicalization of the Freedom in Heidegger's thinking, 'conducted so that the Heideggerian Being as Nothingness and the Schellingian Freedom as a faculty of good and evil fecundate each other', but such a philosophical project encounters an obstacle that in my opinion is insuperable *philosophically* since it overlays spheres of Freedom that differ from each other. Considering the original ontological Freedom as the first Beginning, as eruption, sudden choice that precisely in the act through which it affirms itself is in a direct relationship with a *negativity*, it can be identified by Pareyson as 'an energy that transforms quiescent Nothingness into a dynamic Nothingness', nevertheless for Pareyson this act coincides in Schelling (but not only in Schelling) with a positive vision of Freedom that has experimented and conquered the negation, positing itself as victor over Nothingness and over Evil. According to Pareyson, although Heidegger had realized there was an intimate relationship between ontological Freedom and Nothingness, he could not draw from this realization an adequate and overall comprehension of the question of Freedom, due to his non-Christian or even anti-Christian position. Having accepted the idea that everything depends on Freedom, raising it, in connection with the creation, to the centre and the origin of being as an eminently Christian and not a Greek concept (since the classic freedom of thought is to be understood only in its practical-political sense), and given that Heidegger's philosophy, and above all his approach to Schelling, is mainly linked to the Greek tradition, he could not have gathered the true meaning of his insight in comparing Freedom to Nothingness: 'only Christianity', writes Pareyson, 'could have suggested to Heidegger the centrality of Freedom as a faculty of good and evil' and could have emphasized the negative (evil) 'positivity' of Nothingness.

> Heidegger does speak of the negative, of negation, of negativity, to the point where he characterises being itself as Nothingness. But this 'Nothingness' essentially means the reserve of being not to be confused with the entities and not be a negativity like that of evil, which is a destructive negation, true destructiveness.[2]

But precisely that which Pareyson accuses Heidegger of is in my opinion the true added value of his approach to the question of Schelling's ontological Freedom, which goes well beyond the faculty of good and evil, if only because the two extremes axiologically qualify themselves as such only after the ontological organization and structuring, which is possible – as I said – on the basis of a free conflictual dynamic as the impossible grounding of Being. It is probable – and I say this only as a hypothesis to be verified elsewhere – that precisely Heidegger's 'classic' formulation contributes (unfortunately, given the course it later takes) more than the Christian one to an understanding of the concept of ontological Freedom set out in Schelling's work and which I intend to directly link to, if not overlay with, the original and permanent Conflict of the *Physis*, without it inevitably falling, as Heidegger would have it, in the 'history of being' and its metaphysics.

The concept of Nothingness as the 'standing-reserve' of being, which Heidegger introduced during the 1929 conference, perfectly agrees, in my opinion, with the ontology of Schelling's later work and with the originality of his Idealism, always supported by the idea of a real ('natural') base but totally consumable in the ideal (of the 'spiritual') and capable in its permanent and conflictual dynamics (in its taking the shape of the *Being*) of perpetuating and preserving the possible and many forms of being. The original conflictuality of being resists its reduction to the forms of the history of being and, for Heidegger, as *Ereignis* in its indefinable 'giving', it shows a free and elusive origin (the *Es* of *Es gibt*) which, although it remains as the unexhausted source of being, avoids any form of onto-theology and thus like Schelling's *unvordenkliches Seyn* recognizes itself as such only through the process activated, that is through the '*gibt*' of '*Es gibt*' (the *give* of *it gives*).

Moreover, in Schelling as in Heidegger the relationship with the being of man is not lost nor is the essential relationship of the ontological freedom in its practical-political translation, since the *Dasein* of man lives, in Schelling's philosophy, the double life (infinite and finite) of the Absolute and perceives the Nothingness of its finiteness and at the same time the possibility of 'returning to being the beginning of everything' (with his *Mitwissenschaft* of creation) in that same *anxiety* that, in Heidegger's philosophy, constitutes at first (in *Sein und Zeit*), inasmuch as it is a 'fundamental affective situation', the opening of the being as presence and, therefore, after 1929, the possibility (for the being as presence) of the 'transcendence' in the direction of Being: of the Being that, happening in the *Ereignis*, places being and man (being and thinking) in a sort of 'reciprocal original appropriation'.

> Anxiety, we say, 'one feels uncanny'. What is 'it' that makes 'one' feel uncanny? We cannot say what it is before which one fells uncanny. As a whole it is so for one. All things and we ourselves sink into indifference (*Gleichgültigkeit*). This, however, not in the sense of mere disappearance. Rather, in their very receding, things turn toward us. The receding of beings as a whole, closing in on us in anxiety, oppresses us. We can get no hold on things. In the slipping away of beings only this 'no hold on things' comes over us and remains. Anxiety makes manifest the Nothingness.[3]

But since the Nothingness is revealed in the anxiety and anxiety cannot be a permanent state of mind – rather it occurs only in rare moments, since first of all and in general the Nothingness 'in its originalness is hidden from us' – we are continually immersed in the consideration of the entity (being as presence). The hiddenness in which the Nothingness remains is however functional to its most important meaning, since in its *nullification*, the Nothingness refers us precisely to the entity; in fact, the nullification (*Nichtung*) of the Nothingness cannot be considered an annihilation, nor as a negation of the logical-formal nature: it is rather a 'postponing, thrusting it, to the entity in its totality which vanishes'. Even in Heidegger's rather obscure language we can see that the Nothingness is the essential condition for being as existent, since 'it vanishes' in its elusive totality and it shows itself after all as a non-being contrasted with *Being inasmuch as it is the being of* Nothingness, that is to say 'Being beyond beings (as entities)', and here Heidegger begins using the term 'transcendence'. Starting from the conference *Was ist Metaphysik?*, Heidegger defines as 'transcendence' that which in *Sein und Zeit* he described as 'opening to the being present towards its true capability of being'. Only inasmuch as the being present 'transcends', that is it remains immersed from the start in the Nothingness, can it relate to the entity and to itself: 'without the original manifestness of the Nothingness', writes Heidegger in the 1929 Conference, 'there is no being oneself, nor a *freedom*'. However, while this freedom cannot be summarized in terms of *Sein und Zeit* as an authentic capacity for forward-thinking that the being can enact starting from the decision that anticipates death, it can nevertheless, in my opinion, be traced to a much more general sphere of an eminently ontological nature, since it no longer concerns only the forward-thinking of the being, but rather the original and permanent condition of Being as such. It is not however an initial state, put aside once and for all, but rather a continual *dynamics* from which Being incessantly comes in all its many forms. The ancient theory according to which *ex nihilo nihil fit* (Nothingness comes from Nothingness) is clarified by Heidegger through the enunciation *ex nihilo omne ens qua ens fit* (from the Nothingness all beings as beings come to be), and, in 'transcendence', the being sees that inexhaustible source as the absolute position of the being as becoming. Here we can see what I consider the proximity to Schelling's ontological Freedom, as it was described in *Philosophical Investigations* and then, even more clearly, in the Erlangen conferences. Being, in its transcendence, is allowed to see the anxiety of that Nothingness from which everything that is (inasmuch as it exists) comes. Nevertheless, in Heidegger we read that beyond the finite knowledge of the being, the being occurs always and in any case ('the Nothingness uninterruptedly nullifies, without our being able, with the knowledge we employ in our daily life, really knowing that this is happening') in a free becoming that can never be totally resolved in the knowledge of being. This aspect is also present in the ontology of the later Schelling, highlighted by Manfred Frank, and I feel that this idea can contribute, albeit while taking into consideration all the thematic and argumentative differences, to clarifying the affinity that we see between Schelling's Absolute and Heidegger's *Ereignis*. In the discourse Schelling centred on the relationship between the self-aware subject and the purely existing being, Frank emphasizes the non-objectual (*urständliches*) that makes possible the existence of the Subject which is always like an μη όv:

> In fact, Schelling (referring to Plato and Plutarch) ontologically defines the self-conscious subject as an μη όv. Now an μη όv – unlike a oὐκ όv – is not a *non*-being, that is to say something that in no way can be called existent; the μη όv is rather, as Schelling says, simply not *existent*, or is not *the Existent itself*. Rather, it has a parasitic relationship with the Existent: as a 'relatively' Existent, which borrows its 'being' from the *true Existent*; since from this it has 'been' in the transitive sense [...]
>
> With the expression 'be in the transitive sense' we therefore mean that the non-objectual Subject (not grammatical, as in the quotation above, but rather the Subject of the conscience inasmuch as it *is* object) 'has been' from verbal (but made nominal) Being (in the sense of existing), that is to say it is kept in its partiality [...]
>
> Schelling thus clarifies the way of being of the transitive Being, for which he finds no specific indication in German, and so turns to Arabic. Here the copula 'is' takes the accusative, as in German with the verb *können*, so in Arabic instead of '*homo est sapiens*' it would be '*homo est sapientem*'. Applied to the relation, which takes the existential Being to the purely essential conscience (*wesend*), we should say that in it the Being takes the subject in the accusative sense thus bringing it to appearance.[4] Further proof of this transitive meaning of the existential Being 'Only the pure existent can be that which Being is' [...].[5]
>
> In a lesson from 1833 Schelling states, 'the *grounding* is not existent with respect to *that of which it is* grounding,' (Schelling 1972, 440) – that is only if 'grounding' is seen as the grounding of conscience. Inasmuch as it is the grounding for which the objectual Being shows itself to the conscience (or appears to it), the conscience itself is simply referred to the Being, that is to say it *is not* the Being itself (Kant would say: it is simply a relative, not absolute, position of its object). Elsewhere, in the same cycle of lessons

Schelling says, 'That which simply knows [or the subjective] is precisely therefore the not-Being all the same. To this not-Being all the same, to that which simply knows, on the other hand, only the positive infinite ['the pure Being'] can correspond' (loc. cit., 310 ff.). Schelling also defines the purely Existent Being as 'objectual' and the purely Essential (*das rein Wesende*) as the original 'non-objectual' Being (*das urständliche Sein*) (loc. cit., 408; *SW* I/10, 133). According to this linguistic distinction, that is the fact that without the 'purely objectual' Being, the pure 'non-objectual and original subject, becomes a *Non*-Being, an οὐκ ὄν or a *rien*'.[6]

As Frank himself observes, referring to his book published in 1975 (*Der unendliche Mangel an Sein*), Schelling had already dealt with this form of *ontological excess* in his philosophy of Identity, insisting on 'the independence of its principle [that is] of the so-called absolute Identity of the two *relata* united by the same Identity',[7] which should consist of the *Being* of the Absolute: an ontological independence that cannot ever be reduced to a similarity of ideas (which in the sphere of philosophy of Identity, and in continuity with the critical-Fichtean tradition were simply described by observation).

This *ontological excess* was later translated into the *Indifference* of the *Ungrund* of *Philosophical Investigations*, not by chance defined by Schelling as the 'Absolute *as such*'. This *Being* of the Absolute which coincides, beforehand, with the single unity of the Being of absolute Identity (probably introduced by Schelling after the essay *Of the I as a Principle of Philosophy* also inspired by Hölderlin[8]) and, afterwards, with the *unvordenkliches Seyn* of positive philosophy, has within it a 'force' capable of *commanding* the being (in the verbal sense), thus establishing the fundamental commessure (*Seinsfuge*) that allows the distinction between subject and object and the relative finite forms of being: this force is described in dynamic terms as '*Wollen*' and, in ontological terms, by means of the particular use that Schelling makes of the 'copula' as Being that *allows* the being, that is *it is* the being in the transitive sense.

In my opinion, Frank's discourse can be extended to the entire ontological sphere and should not be limited to the question of the Subject, inasmuch as it is a μη όν made possible in its reality (in its passage to being) by the *transitivity* of Being; the Being of the Absolute that *can* the being of the conciliation of the 'relations of thought' (and it is however always beyond this as an inexhaustible reserve) and finally that absolute and original Freedom that *stands* (beyond the onto-theology) as the impossible grounding of everything, as the permanent and dynamic principle of being. From here the idea of a dynamic that *commands* the ontology, since it is only starting from this that it is possible to define, for example:

1) the subject as a μη όν opposed to the *Being* of the Absolute;
2) the *unprethinakble being (das unvordenkliche Seyn)* as the purely contingent;
3) the cause that it opposes as *what simply can be (das Seynkönnende).*

To translate my statement into Heideggerian language we could say that:

> *The* Es *of the* Es gibt *can be compared to the Indifference of the Un-grund, to the Absolute as such, to the* unvordenkliches Seyn *(the purely contingent), but all this could be explained only in the 'giving', i.e. in the 'making happen'; that is to say only after (a posteriori), in the dynamics of the process that develops: from the* Es *we immediately pass to the* gibt!

2 Being as *Physis*?

The description of the *unvordenkliches Seyn* as 'purely contingent' allows Schelling to present a dynamic, physical Principle (from the Greek term φύσις that Heidegger translates, in his *Introduction to Metaphysics*, as 'permanent imposing and hatching self', *das aufgehend-verweilende Walten*), which, realizing itself only through the opposition of *what simply can be*, certainly overcomes the limits of an onto-theological principle (inasmuch as the *grounding* always denies itself as such), and at the same time preserves an *ontological excess* (the inexpressible *Being* of the Absolute) which, remaining extraneous to the process and, being able to 'choose' to pass to the process or to abstain from it, makes the aforementioned Principle capable of persisting in time, guaranteeing, in the becoming, the possibility of every *new* free beginning.

The theoretical reasons for Heidegger's resistance to overlaying his *Ereignis* on Schelling's Absolute, which I explained at the start of this chapter, probably lie in the Heideggerian idea that Schelling does not in fact overcome 'the history that thinks being starting from a grounding', but remains substantially with a concept that posits the φύσις as the ontological grounding of being.

> Seen in a more original manner this fundamental trait of his philosophy [i.e. Schelling's passage to the 'Positive', which for Heidegger precedes inasmuch as it is *Ungrund* every possible duality and contrast[9]], without knowing it, goes to the φύσις-ἀλήθεια, to the clarifying itself and the persisting in self; to the initially and correctly thus defined *Ex-sistierendes*, that originated from itself. Nevertheless, and this is decisive, Schelling sees only that reason cannot be brought into play here as *pre*-thinking, although blindly, that is to say that here it must simply welcome, accept. He does not however seek the ἀλήθεια and the essential permanence (*Wesung*) of these essences as οὐσία; he seeks the present in its being present – the existence (*Dasein*) in the common meaning.[10]

Nevertheless, Schelling's Absolute as such can be described as φύσις only when the latter is read, in close connection with the Nothingness of the Beginning, in the sense of origin, source of Being: an inexhaustible origin that escapes, in its elusive dynamics, with the being to which it gives itself in all its forms and determinations. In Schelling's overall plan, the Absolute cannot in fact be seen simply as the totality of the being (and already in this it goes beyond the metaphysical concept), which posits itself and knows itself persisting in its position (*Setzung*).[11] The fact that in the epistemological sphere the idea of totality is historically (that is in the 'history of being') defined as impossible marks an impossibility which is first of all of an ontological nature, since the Schellingian Absolute (but actually any honest attempt to consider the Absolute in post-metaphysical terms) is not merely the totality of the existent since it is possibly always becoming and moreover is permanently connected to the absolutely free Principle from which it comes.

Beginning from the hidden dynamics of this Principle which is only clarified speculatively and only *a posteriori* in the supra-relation to Nothingness, which 'characterizes' that ontological excess from which it takes its cue, we understand how Schelling's Absolute can be read as φύσις: that is to say as a *Nature* that 'lets (*makes*)' the various forms of being 'be', through its *dynamis*; that is after all as an *original and permanent dynamics that commands an ontology*.

Heidegger clarifies how originally the term φύσις, as a general character of being,[12] indicated 'the emerging-abiding-prevailing and the persistence dominated in it. In this emerging-prevailing are included both the "becoming" and the "being" in the narrow sense of the immovable permanence' (*Introduction to Metaphysics*).[13] But as he observes in his essay 'On the essence and concept of φύσις', it 'is the presencing of the absencing of itself, one that is on-the-way from itself and unto itself'.[14] As he affirms – commenting on the poem *Wie wenn am Feiertage* by Hölderlin – what is thus defined as 'nature' is at the same time the 'sacred' (*das Heilige*): inasmuch as φύσις is the 'rising in the open, the lifting and illumination of the *Lichtung*, which is the only place it can appear',[15] it is above God and the gods, it – 'the powerful' – is still capable of something other than the gods: only 'in it, inasmuch as it is *Lichtung*, can every thing be present'.[16] In this consists the 'sacredness' of Nature, this emerging to the entities, guarding them in its embrace.

In manifesting the entities, the φύσις is not reduced to them nor to their totality; it also remains the source and the becoming that accompanies the entities to their manifestation while remaining hidden: As stated in fragment 123 of Heraclitus, cited by Porphyry, 'nature loves to hide'.

Self-hiding belongs to the predilection [*Vor-liebe*] of being; i.e., it belongs to that within which being has secured its essence. And the essence of being is to unconceal itself, to emerge, to come out into the unhidden – φύσις. Only what in its very essence *unconceals* [*ent-birgt*] and must unconceal itself, can love to conceal itself be. Only what is unconcealing can be concealing. And therefore the *kriptesthai* of φύσις is not to be overcome, not to be stripped from φύσις. Rather, the task is the much more difficult one of allowing the φύσις, in all the purity of its essence, the *kriptesthai* that belongs to it.[17]

That is to say, to definitely grasp the *Ereignis* of being while at the same time welcoming its *Enteignis*.

Being based on the Nothingness of the original freedom that resists being and that stands not simply as μη όν, which would mean accepting the theory of a power (a relative Nothingness) that acts and is finally destined to die out, but as ούκ όν, the Schellingian Absolute cannot be read in the metaphysical terms to which Heidegger's interpretation relegates it.

Although he recognizes that Schelling, with his positive philosophy, goes well beyond the Hegelian 'rationalism', Heidegger seems to want to trace the Schellingian Positive to the mere entity that is present and is perceived.[18] Heidegger recognizes that the elusive origin of the 'positive' lies in *Freedom*, since in reading Schelling's *Another Deduction of the Principles of Positive Philosophy*, he states that (before the free will of the Godhead, inasmuch as it is *necessary nature*) the opposition of *what simply can be* to the *unvordenkliches Seyn* is possible only thanks to the 'will of the absolutely Free' and this reality (*Wirklichkeit*), which precedes every possibility, cannot be thought *a priori* (that is to say through rational philosophy) but rather starting from eternity.[19]

Such freedom cannot, however, be seen as the freedom of an entity, nor as the freedom of the Supreme Entity, which is given only at a later time, but as absolute Freedom, which permits the opposition to the *unvordenkliches Seyn* and therefore the power and the concrete existence of that which constitutes the 'ultimate essence' of that dynamic Principle, that Schelling means to present in his speculation beyond every relapse *on this side* of the so-called onto-theology.

As I have said, this Freedom can only be indissolubly linked to Nothingness, since only in this supra-relation can there be the dynamics that derives from it, and, apart from the various determinations of being, only in it is it possible for that extreme definition of being *as* Nothingness mentioned by Schelling in the *Exposition of Philosophical Empiricism* to exist, which is, after all the nub of the Heideggerian conference of 1929.

At the end of the text I have just mentioned, Schelling deals with the question of the *creatio ex nihilo* moving the question of the supra-ontological sphere, which precedes the Godhead itself, backwards and thus introducing, alongside the distinction between the μη ὄν and the οὐκ ὄν, a third defined as the 'non-existent' (*material informis*): *das Unseyende*, that is to say 'that which must not be, inasmuch as it is [...] the blind and unlimited being that must *ever more* be eliminated through creation'.[20]

If the μη ὄν is that which is as present, in the sense that only the *effective, real* (*wirkliches*) being is excluded from it, while in it persists the possibility of being, then the οὐκ ὄν is, instead, that 'from which not only the *reality* of being is excluded, but also being in general, and therefore also the possibility'. Since the definition of οὐκ ὄν does not allow any passage to being and that of μη ὄν shows that being is already contained within it, though in the form of power, Schelling introduces, as I have said, the *material informis* ('which also the supporters of creation from Nothingness establish as the basis for the creation of that which has form and figure') as a 'non-existent': as that which in itself must not become being, but needs a power that is opposed to it. However, the 'non-existent' (the real principle B) thus introduced assumes the characteristics of a μη ὄν, since, to some extent, being is already contained within it, although it does not (yet) present itself as the real being. Schelling must therefore recognize that this mere presupposition of the creation must be able in turn to derive from a vacuum, from an absolute Nothingness that precedes it:

the true doctrine of the creation from Nothingness thus also recognizes this *Néant*, this Nothingness (this *material informis*), but as something that in turn was born from Nothingness (*de rien*); it constitutes for that doctrine the immediate possibility of the real Being, but the doctrine itself does not admit that this power existed in any way before.[21]

The problematic conclusion of the *Exposition of Philosophical Empiricism* (1836) in effect introduces us to the over-realistic theory of *Another Deduction of the Principles of Positive Philosophy* (a text that presumably dates from 1839): while the opposition presented in *Exposition of Philosophical Empiricism* between the unlimited real principle (B) and the ideal principle (A) requires the position of a *real Being* that precedes this contrast, the latter can certainly not be deduced through that opposition that it allows and ensures, preceding it ontologically. It is therefore necessary to go *beyond* being inasmuch as it is a product of that essential contrast between the two opposing principles, in a sphere that, however, can only be described as οὐκ ὄν: that is as that which *is not* in any way. The impossible concept encountered by Schelling is that same *Ungrund* of *Philosophical Investigations*, that is to say 'the Positive that precedes every contrast or duality'. As I have said, this concept (which already in 1809 Schelling saw as intimately connected with 'Nothingness', or distinct from it) was further investigated by Schelling, in the years of positive philosophy, through the definition of *unvordenkliches Seyn* as 'purely[22] contingent': a definition that became possible as such only in the act of opposition to *what simply can be* and in the subsequent development of the dynamic process, and which before that dynamic stood as the *absolute Nothingness* (οὐκ ὄν).

The Nothingness of the Beginning is therefore that *Being* of the Absolute as such which in fact allows the dynamic of the beginning, of the origin and guarantees its permanence inasmuch as it is an inexhaustible 'reserve' for the being produced by the opposition. The οὐκ ὄν, that we can describe only through 'speculative' hypotheses – which belongs to positive philosophy – is therefore the unprethinkable sphere of the original ontological Freedom, which allows the multiple and successive forms of being and appears already and always as *Being* (absolutely) *real or overreal*[23]: a Beginning that is such only after *having been so* in total freedom (therefore on the impossible 'grounding' of Nothingness) and which – the true qualifying aspect of the Schellingian Principle – remains free to re-present itself at any time in the process that it activates, as a sudden and unexpected eruption, which pierces the continuity of the development and can (*historically*) burst in to show the necessary *falseness* of the *unities* (*as beings as presence*) that it constitutes and determines.

3 Being and Knowledge: The transitive meaning of Being

In the Erlangen conferences of 1821 it becomes clear that the Principle '[is not] a principle only at the beginning, to then cease being so, but that which everywhere and always at the beginning, in the middle and at the end, is equally a principle',[24] and Schelling also shows what he means by the abyssal ontological freedom that 'grounds' being in all its various forms, including the *verbal* form. In his *living* System we are clearly not seeking a propositional principle (*Grund-satz*), but rather a Subject 'which runs throughout and does not persist in anything', that is to say a 'simply indefinable' *Being* (in the first instance a Nothingness) which, however, allows the formulation of judgements expressed in the verbal form (from the copula) without being able to wholly come down to it.

> Not that it is not something, which would at least be a negative definition; but neither is it Nothingness, since it is instead everything. It alone is nothing inasmuch as it is single, immobile, particular; it is B, C, D, and so on, only inasmuch as each of these points belongs to the flow of the indivisible movement. There is nothing else that it is and there is nothing that it is not. It is incessant movement, it cannot be enclosed in any form, it is incoercible, elusive, truly infinite.[25]

Schelling identifies ontological Freedom as the essence of the absolute Subject (*Urstand*) as that which, in its coessential unity with Nothingness (original and permanent), can manifest being in all its forms, without, however, persisting in any. Through the concept of (eternal[26]) *Mögen*, which in German preserves the composite meaning of to be able to (*Können*) and will (*Wollen*), Schelling describes the dynamic of the principle of his *living* System, that although it does not coincide with knowledge (*Wissen*), which occupies only the rational-negative sphere, it guarantees the possibility thanks to the *verbal* meaning of being and yet remains beyond it as *Weisheit* (wisdom): that is to say as the eternal freedom of the Absolute which is *efficient knowledge*, active and living knowledge (and in this sense it *commands* being in all its definite and definable forms), in which the power and the force are preserved in unity, 'since it [the wisdom] is that which is in everything, but precisely for this reason, also in that which is above everything'.[27]

Although the description that Schelling offers of the *eternal Mögen* – 'eternal freedom, eternal potency to will [...] not the potency to will of something, but potency to will itself, that is the eternal *Magie*'[28] – may seem to be an etymologically interesting formulation (though substantially vague and lacking in theoretical content), it acquires a totally different and central meaning when this concept is read critically in the context in which it is presented: that is within the umpteenth attempt by Schelling to approach the possibility of the Principle of a System *living* in knowledge, knowledge that is always expressed in the form of judgement guaranteed by the 'copula' which rests on a superior (dialectic) concept of Identity. Moreover, we must not forget that *Mögen* comes to integrate the concept of *Wollen*,[29] which in itself could erroneously generate (as after all occurred in the history of the reception of Schelling's thinking, also thanks to Heidegger's reading) the idea that it served as a metaphysical (onto-theological) principle to explain the totality of being, in the super relation that intends to 'describe' the undefinable, or the *Being* (in its many meanings) of the Absolute.[30]

In holding together the potency to do (*Können*) and the will (*Wollen*) in their purity,[31] the *Mögen* describes (in a 'pure will' lacking in knowledge since it precedes all objecthood and therefore all *form*) the dynamic *eternal* of the absolutely free decision for/of the Beginning which gives *life* to the System of knowledge: a dynamic that Schelling would subsequently consider metaphysical and therefore, with respect to the misunderstood concept of φύσις-ἀλήθεια, that which, persisting in itself, opens to understanding, clarifying itself in an absolute coincidence of being and knowledge and making use of the *purely contingent unvordenkliches Seyn*.

> This magic [from *Mögen*], until it becomes efficient, is = tranquil knowledge. Becoming efficient, enclosing itself in a form [by means of the *Being* of the Absolute which *in the transitive sense commands* the forms of being and their verbal relation], it becomes aware, it attempts a knowledge, and thus proceeds from form to form, passes from one knowledge to another, but only in order to open the way that takes it back to the beatitude of not knowing, which thus becomes an awareness of not-knowing (*ein Wissendes Nichtwissen*). This movement is therefore a generator of science (naturally here we do not mean human science).[32]

The 'movement' that generates science (and which institutes the overall *ontological* system and therefore the consequent epistemological structure) is thus guaranteed by the dynamic of the *eternal Mögen*, which, being forced to translate itself into the forms of being and therefore also into knowledge, ensured by the 'copula' in the judgement, is 'based' on the superior concept of Identity, as the co-belonging of the different (from Being and from Nothingness), and it becomes the permanent and absolutely free Principle of the *Being* of the Absolute. It stands, in its intimate overreal relation with Nothingness[33] (as οὐκ ὄν), as (1) a guarantee of the various forms of being, that is to say the inexhaustible 'reserve' of being; (2) the impossible 'free grounding', or as the essential (superreal) conflict between freedom and the need for being to develop in all its forms; and (3) as an *absolute position* that assures and institutes, on the basis of the 'dialectic' concept of Identity, the *relative being* of the predication.

I have said that on the topic of being in a *transitive sense* Manfred Frank has carried out very useful investigations (including comparing the Schellingian texts to the results of Sartre's ontology of *Being and Nothingness, L'Être et le Néant*) verifying how this approach to being rests substantially on the Schellingian concept of the absolute and the antepredicative Identity of Being. The absolute position of the identitary being, as *Wirklichkeit* which has always preceded the thinking on which it is based (and therefore the sphere described through the Kantian categories), has, so to speak, the availability of the power of being (and therefore of knowledge) which is opposed to it: the *Wirklichkeit* of the absolute Identity is that *unprethinkable being* of positive philosophy which is also described as *potentia potentiae*: that is to say as that (only improperly named) 'power (*Potenz*), that has in its hands the [same] power', while it first among all the possibilities, ontically founds (precisely the 'power') of this δύναμις.[34] The continuity that we find in Schelling between the antepredicative *Being* of the absolute Identity and the *unprethinkable being* makes it possible to deal with the *transitive* meaning of Being on the basis of the concept of the 'copula' which matured in Schelling already at the time of the *Würzburger System* (1804) and then, more clearly, in *Aphorismen zur Einleitung in die Naturphilosophie*, 1806 (*Aphorisms as an Introduction to the Philosophy of Nature*). The ontological idea that appears at the peak of the philosophy of Identity is taken up again, although only incidentally, in the *Philosophical Investigations* of 1809: here Schelling, in an attempt to clarify how the question of authentic pantheism can only rest on the original Freedom, shows how the question cannot be dealt with as a simply *theo*-logical problem, but is above all an *ontological* question, based on a *dialectic* perception of the principle of Identity. This aspect is also well highlighted by Heidegger in the *Vorlesung* on Schelling's freedom in 1936, where he clarifies that pantheism is to be considered an ontological question and how it appears incomprehensible only to those who – as Schelling observes – persist 'in the general misunderstanding of the law of identity or the meaning of the copula in the judgement'. Heidegger correctly observes that Schelling poses the ontological question of the concept of being starting from the meaning of the copula 'is' and consequently, since the copula of the judgement is a constitutive element of the proposition (of the predication in general), the proposition becomes 'the *Leitmotiv*' of the ontological question, starting from the principle of Identity. This principle should obviously not be read in the 'common' sense of selfness or sameness, since this prevents adequate understanding of Identity: the co-belonging of the subject and the predicate does not expend its entire meaning, which should rather be seen also and above all in its dialectic meaning of the 'co-belonging of the different in the one' or as 'unity of a unity and of an opposition'.

In the attempt to understand the statement behind pantheism, 'God is all things', we cannot stop at Identity as sameness between God and all things. As Heidegger observes, 'the correct concept of identity means the original co-belonging of the different in one, the one which is at the same time also the foundation of the possibility of the different'. This concept of Identity is defined as 'dialectic' in the sense that it includes a term in its 'passage towards the other, in its essential relation with the other, and not seeing it only in its immediacy'. In this sense Schelling's original identity is not a dead relation of indifferent and sterile sameness; it is the 'unity' and an immediately productive unity, progressing to the other, to a 'creative' unity.[35]

This 'creativity' which Heidegger refers to, describing the (super)relation of Identity, is ontologically affirmed through the *transitive meaning* that Schelling assigns to the superreal being of the absolute Identity, when the *what simply can be* that is opposed to the *unprethinkable being* is no longer considered as itself (as the power of an act), but rather as it *is*, in essential unity with the immemorial being, the purely existent (*das rein Seyende*).

> [This] is the meaning of Is (of the *copula*) in every principle that truly expresses something (that is not tautological). A *is* B means: A is the subject of B. In this we find two things: 1) A is in itself also without B, and could also be something other than B; only inasmuch as A is capable of a being itself, and therefore also of not being = B, we say *cum emphasi*: A is B [...].

But, 2) precisely because it could also be other than B, this being a 'could be something else' with respect to B makes it mere power of possibility of B, and only thus or only in this way it *is* B.

In Arabic Is (the *copula*) is expressed through a word that belongs to German *kann*, 'can'. This is clear from the fact that the in the dialects similar to Arabic, this word means the subject, foundation, founding, determinant. Moreover, only thus can we explain that in contrast to other languages, at least those known to be, in which the verb sum takes the nominative [...] only the Arabs construct it with the accusative.[36]

The particular 'description' of the *copula* is introduced by Schelling in order to clarify the expression according to which, once in unity with the unprethinkable being, 'what simply can be is no longer itself, but *is* purely existent'.

In fact, to think of the *copula* in the *transitive sense* means attributing it the meaning of 'power': the sentence *homo est sapiens* should be read as *homo est sapientem*, so that the accusative indicates that the copula *est* has, in truth, the meaning of *potest*; in this manner, in the proposition '*homo est sapientem*', 'man' is to be seen as the carrier, the subject of 'being wise': 'he is wise inasmuch as he has, in himself, as mere power, the potency to be opposed, he is thus capable of being-wise, he assumes it as his predicate, has power over it'.

By means of the *copula*, the Being of the absolute Identity, inasmuch as it is *what simply can be* in essential unity with the *unprethinkable* being (its *material* power) 'can', is (in the *transitive* meaning) being in all its forms, and it preserves in the Nothingness that always is (and therefore persists as a 'reserve' of being) the possibility of being *different* from the way it is, from the forms in which it appears.

The theory of predication itself, which is based on the 'dialectic' concept of Identity, presupposes in Schelling the original juxtaposition of Nothingness (in the sense of οὐκ ὄν) and that, on the one hand, guarantees the absolute Freedom on which Schelling's ontology is constructed, and, on the other, shows incontrovertibly how the *dynamics* from which Schelling's ontology originates cannot be described exclusively, as Heidegger's simplification would have it, from the metaphysical concept of an Absolute like φύσις-ἀλήθεια, 'as in clarify itself and persist in itself'[37]), since an ontological-dynamic *excess* is introduced into it, which has always preceded the process and, from the absolute Nothingness that it *was*, becomes, thanks to the free dynamic that activates the process itself, the indefinable and permanent 'reserve'[38] for the forms of being. In the sphere of predication, the *copula* preserves the (real) effective dialectic nature of Being, since in the judgement of the principle of Identity it already expresses, on the one hand, the *potential* of being to act as subject for a particular form-predicate and, on the other, the supreme power of being other than the form that, as predicate, it assumes in the judgement. This *power-to-be-other* is certainly that which in the epistemological sphere ensures and guarantees the predication, but it does nothing more than repeat that *excess* which is first of all of an ontological-dynamic nature.[39] which really, effectively (*wirklich*), determines the passage from Nothingness to being. Epistemology does not found Schellingian ontology, but, vice versa, the *ontology* ensures and guarantees the *epistemology*. Moreover, in my reading, the ontological sphere is in turn preceded by the dynamic sphere that allows the dialectic passage from Nothingness to being: only thanks to an absolutely free *dynamic* that allows the passage from the unprethinkable being to the process, is it in fact possible to describe the very first stages of Schellingian ontology, describing the unprethinkable as the *purely contingent* which 'necessarily' (in order that the process may pass to the act and can therefore be 'described' *a posteriori*) is opposed to *what simply can be*. This *dynamic* which is necessarily described *a posteriori* and in a speculative sphere (that of positive philosophy[40]) constitutes the ultimate essence of the Schellingian Principle of the System, inasmuch as it is absolute Freedom of the Beginning: not a simply formal freedom, applied from outside to a process already underway, but rather an essential Freedom, belonging to the Being, which inasmuch as it is existing, real, effective (*wirksam*), coincides with the absolute *Wirklichkeit*.

The problem with the pantheism that Schelling seems to introduce only incidentally at the beginning of *Philosophical Investigations into the Essence of Human Freedom* is in fact the fundamental premise for the entire philosophical project that Schelling undertakes with this writing and for his ontological concept that rests on the *dialectic* literature of the Identity principle which is founded on the copula. The question of pantheism, observes Schelling, is not included in its philosophical meaning only by those who persist 'in the general misunderstanding of the law of identity or the meaning of the copula in the judgment'. That the question of pantheism cannot be simply dealt with as a theological question, but first of all as an ontological question is justified by Schelling through the *dialectic* reading of the *copula* in the law of Identity. As we have seen, this *transitive* reading of the copula substantially repeats the original dynamic of the Principle that although it delivers itself to a form of being, it is not wholly comprised therein and acts as the subject for the able-to-be-different. In this possibility of being different which is always preserved in the *transitive* sense of being, and therefore in the copula in the judgement, lies the impossible foundation of pantheism presented by Schelling, since it is absolute ontological Freedom. It is, in effect, inappropriate to speak of pantheism in Schelling's philosophy since it is not really summarized by the formula 'God is all things' but rather by the superior expression 'the Absolute is all things' ('We must not be afraid of confusing the Absolute – that absolute subject – with God himself [...] The Absolute is above God'[41]).

Now, what we have observed with regard to the Schellingian Absolute prevents us from seeing it in the sense that Heidegger's interpretation assigns to it, that is as φύσις-ἀλήθεια (clarifying itself and persisting in itself). Schelling's philosophical concept of the Absolute cannot in fact be included in the Heideggerian forms of onto-theology 'in the original and essential sense that the conceptual understanding (λόγος, *lógos*) of the entity as a whole poses the question of the foundation of Being and this foundation is called θεός [theós], God',[42] and this clearly not because God has been substituted by the Absolute which in itself could also only be read as a terminological expedient, but rather because the particular ontological idea of the Absolute proposed by Schelling rests on an absolutely free dynamics (inseparably linked to the Nothingness of the Beginning and which constantly repeats itself in the predicative form) which cannot effectively act as a foundation in the sense that onto-theology assigns to it. The absolute and ontological (we can also say *oukontological*) Freedom, given its ineliminable super-relation to Nothingness, *begins* and ensures the being, as its indispensable Principle, which always withdraws from it as grounding.

Therefore, in the formula 'the Absolute *is* all things', in the dialectic and superior sense of the Identity that prevents us from reading the relation as sameness, we can summarize Schelling's *System* of Freedom.[43] as it is initially set out starting with *Philosophical Investigations* and later perfected (without becoming a definitive form that completely satisfied him) in the Erlangen and Berlin lectures.

The *lack* of coincidence between being and knowledge that we find in the System of the Absolute, also through the *transitive* meaning attributed to the copula that presupposes an *intransitive* sphere which persists and does not give itself as knowledge, shows an ontological excess that means Schelling's *Philosophical Investigations* must be read not only and not merely – as Heidegger would wish – as 'the summit of German Metaphysical Idealism', but rather as the turning point in Western philosophy that sees being starting from a grounding.

> The little word 'is', which speaks everywhere in our language, and tells of Being even where It does not appear expressly, contains the whole destiny of Being from the ἔστιν γὰρ εἶναι of Parmenides to the 'is' of Hegel's speculative sentence, and to the dissolution of the 'is' in the positing of the Will to Power with Nietzsche.[44]

Although Schelling is not quoted here, the dissolution of 'is' in the command of the *Will to Power* that Heidegger mentions is undoubtedly to be overlaid – as we have seen – on the *transitive* meaning of being in Schelling's System: this overlapping (which I consider possible and proper for more than one reason) is possible only when we recognize that the sphere of being *commanded* by Nietzsche's Will to Power is not a merely conventional and correlational sphere, but rather an unavoidable necessity, which certainly shows its 'relativity' with respect to the overall nature of the world as Will to Power, but does not therefore completely lose its validity ('*Admitting Being* is necessary in order to be able to think and argue: logic only handles formulas that are valid for that which remains constant'[45]). Nihilism is thinking that the necessarily *false units* produced *in* the being (through the *copula*) can completely exhaust the reality of Being, which instead is always in excess with respect to knowledge. In this sense, if Nietzsche's nihilism shows the limits of metaphysical thinking on the basis of this unsolvable (in knowledge) excess, then we find Schelling's concept on the same path when, in distinguishing between *Wissen* (knowledge) and *Weisheit* (knowledge as the *effective* knowledge that creates) and introducing the *transitive* sense of being, it shows an atopical potential and free space in its will (*das ewige Mögen*), which in intimate connection with the Nothingness of the Beginning commands in the copula the forms of being without ever being able to completely reduce to it.[46] In Heidegger's language, the *transitive* function of being efficaciously shows the meaning of the so-called ontological difference and institutes a super-relation between being and the entity that tries to surpass the confines of metaphysical–onto-theological thinking, which still and always thinks of being starting from the totality and the grounding of the same.

> While we are facing the difference, though by the step back we are already releasing it into that which gives thought, we can say: the Being of beings means Being which is beings. The 'is' here speaks transitively, in transition. Being here becomes present in the manner of a transition to beings. But Being does not leave its own place and go over to beings, as though beings were first with-out Being and could be approached by Being subsequently. Being transits (that), comes unconcealingly over (that) which arrives as something of itself unconcealed only by that coming-over. Arrival means:

to keep concealed in unconcealedness to abide present in this keeping to be a being.⁴⁷

This does not mean, for Heidegger, that the Being abandons so to speak its place to completely transfer itself to the entity: rather, the being 'passes through' the entity and shows itself as the *handing on (Überkommnis)* that reveals, and the entity thus appears in the modality of the *arrival (Ankunft)* 'that hides-saves itself in the speed':

> Being in the sense of unconcealing overwhelming, and beings as such in the sense of arrival that keeps itself concealed, are present, and thus differentiated, by virtue of the Same, the differentiation. That differentiation alone grants and holds apart the 'between', in which the overwhelming and the arrival are held toward one another, are borne away from and toward each other. The difference of Being and beings, as the differentiation of overwhelming and arrival, is the perdurance (*Austrag*) of the two in *unconcealing keeping in concealment*. Within this perdurance there prevails a clearing of what veils and closes itself off – and this its prevalence bestows the being apart, and the being toward each other, of overwhelming and arrival.⁴⁸

In Heidegger's 'ontological difference' the problem of thinking the relation between Being and entity in the metaphysical terms of foundation-founder and founded can still be seen. In order to avoid this reading, which is still clearly onto-theological, Heidegger describes the divergence (*Austrag*) as a circling (*ein Kreisen*), in an extraordinary affinity – in my opinion – with the theoretical conclusions of Schelling and Nietzsche who, highlighting the same danger (and thus already placing themselves at the turning point of Western thinking), use the figure of the circle that turns back on itself and is therefore saved from the position of being as definitive and final *Grund* (e.g. the circularity introduced in Schelling's *Weltalter* and the *doctrine of the eternal recurrence of the same*).

> Inasmuch as Being becomes present as the Being of beings, as the difference, as perduration, the separateness and mutual relatedness of grounding and of

accounting for endures, Being grounds beings, and beings, as what *is* most of all, account for Being. One comes over the other, one arrives in the other. Overwhelming and arrival appear in each other in reciprocal reflection. Speaking in terms of the difference, this means: perdurance is a circling, the circling of Being and beings around each other (*das Umeinanderkreisen von Sein und Seiendem*).[49]

Now, in this circling of being around the entity and vice versa, a fundamental role is played by the *Nothingness*: the only ontological difference is in fact described by Heidegger as 'the *non* between Being and the existent'; if the Nothingness as a 'reserve' of being did not breach this game of returns between Being and the entity, we would be dealing with a finite circle traceable to knowledge (i.e. the description of the movement of Hegel's *Begriff*). Nonetheless, in Heidegger too – although it is not explained in these terms – we see an ontological excess that prevents this conclusion and which, on the contrary, avails itself of a dynamics never determinable that is described by the event/appropriation (*das Ereignis*). As we have seen, in fact, in the *Ereignis* as event-appropriation there is at the same time the *Enteignis*, that is the ex-propriation: the essence of the truth, besides coinciding with the manifestation of the entities, coincides also with the manifestation of what is hidden, of what is not manifested, that is, with the dynamic-ontological excess that does not come to knowledge.

We have seen that in the 'making happen' of the *Ereignis* (and therefore in the already-happened) a Nothingness, from which the being that has been made to occur, is highlighted: the *Es* of *Es gibt* (the *it* of *it gives*), which we have read in theoretical continuity with the *Un-grund* and with the *unvordenkliches Seyn* of Schelling's work. In particular this last Schellingian concept, since it is described (always and only *a posteriori*) as the *purely* contingent, shows such an affinity with Nothingness (as οὐκ ὄν and not as μὴ ὄν, which in the Schellingian discourse would mean re-encountering the difficulties proper to the *Weltalter*[50] and thus sinking back into the sphere of being in power) as to take shape as the extreme attempt to exceed the boundaries of metaphysical thinking in the Heideggerian sense of the attribute. Precisely this affinity with Nothingness positively characterizes, in my opinion, the attempt made by Heidegger with the introduction of the *Ereignis* to elaborate a way of thinking that on the one hand comprises the coincidence of being and (onto-theological) thinking on being and, on the other, knows how to 'show' a vacuum from which the coincidence and this excess continually derive.

In this sense the 'sameness' of thinking and being, already introduced by Parmenides, is explained by Heidegger as co-belonging to both, 'being and thought belong to both', states Heidegger in *Identity and Difference*, 'an identity whose essence derives from that co-belonging that we call event [*Ereignis*]'. Although the *Ereignis* is not in itself an abyss or a vacuum, it presupposes in its dynamics – since it is not resolved in a relation between being and thought – a super-relation between Being and Nothingness on the basis of a superior Identity which *can* (make happen) the being in its co-belonging to knowledge; precisely in this direction, there is a possible perspective for reading the 'essence of truth' in *Contributions to Philosophy*:

> 228. *The essence of truth and non-truth*
>
> This statement – deliberately formulated as self-contradictory – is to state that what has the character of nothing (*das Nichtafte*) belongs to truth, but by no means only as a lack, rather as what withstands, that self-sheltering-concealing that comes into the clearing (*Lichtung*) as such.
>
> Thereby the original relation of truth to being as event (*Ereignis*) is grasped. Nevertheless, that statement is risky in its intention of bringing the strange essential sway of truth nearer by such estrangement.
>
> Understood completely originally, there lies in that statement the most essential insight into – and at the same time allusion of – the inner intimacy and contentiousness in being itself as event.[51]

The essence of the truth is therefore in the 'not' of the truth of the *Ereignis*, since it always gives to the mere (active) *negation* of any grounding or presupposition. Precisely so that being can find the essence of the truth as freedom it is necessary for being to give itself as *Ereignis* in its insoluble and coessential relation to Nothingness, which (although concealed and forgotten in the persistent consideration of being) persists in every moment of being: '*der Anfang*', writes Heidegger, '*ist das Seyn selbst als Ereignis*', that is the beginning is the being itself as *Ereignis*, but this does not mean that the *Ereignis* constitutes the beginning as the historical, original fact of being, as it also means that the *Ereignis*, in its coessential relation to Nothingness, as *negation* of every presupposition including its 'past' (the being-already-given) is always constituted as a possible *new beginning*,[52] thus repeating the inexhaustible dynamic of Schelling's Absolute.

NOTES

Introduction

1 See E. C. Corriero, 'Schelling Again', in *Rivista di Estetica*, forthcoming in 2020.

2 On the continuity between the philosophy of nature and positive philosophy, see E. C. Corriero, 'The Ungrounded Nature of Being: Grounding a Dynamic Ontology, From Philosophy of Nature to Positive Philosophy', in *Kabiri* (2018), pp. 17–35.

3 F. W. J. Schelling, *Sämmtliche Werke*, Stuttgart: Cotta Verlag, 1856–1861 [SW], SW, I/7, p. 356.

4 Compare M. Ferraris and M. De Caro, *Introduzione a Bentornata realtà. Il nuovo realismo in discussione* (*Introduction to Welcome Back Reality: New Realism Discussed*), edited by M. De Caro and M. Ferraris, Turin: Einaudi, 2012, p. VI.

5 *Bentornata realtà?* (*Welcome Back Reality?*)

6 This is how Massimo Cacciari expresses it: 'Schelling still represents the "mystery" of the philosophy of *krisis*, that is, of the thought that claims to go beyond that fulfilment of philosophy that classical idealism wanted to represent', in M. Cacciari, 'Schelling postumo' ('Posthumous Schelling'), Preface to E. C. Corriero, *Vertigini della ragione. Schelling e Nietzsche* (*The Vertigo of Reason: Schelling and Nietzsche*), Turin: Rosenberg & Sellier, 2018 (2nd edn), p. 17.

7 Q. Meillassoux, *Après la finitude. Essai sur la nécessité de la contingence*, Paris: Editions de Seuil, 2006; *After Finitude. An Essay on the Contingency of Necessity*, London and New York: Continuum, 2008, p. 5.

8 SW II/3, p. 162.

9 To use an expression from Meillassoux, according to whom 'any reality anterior to the emergence of the human species – or even anterior to every recognized form of life on earth' can be defined 'ancestral' (Meillassoux, *After Finitude*, p. 10).

10 Ibid., p. 8.

11 'The appropriation appropriates man and Being to their essential togetherness. In the frame, we glimpse a first, oppressing flash of the appropriation. The frame constitutes the active nature of the modern world of technology. In the frame we witness a belonging together of man and Being in which the letting belong first determines the manner of the "together" and its unity. We let Parmenides's fragment "For the Same are thinking as well as Being" introduce us to the question of a belonging together in which belonging has precedence over "together". The question of the meaning of

this Same is the question of the active nature of identity. The doctrine of metaphysics represents identity as a fundamental characteristic of Being. Now it becomes clear that Being belongs with thinking to an identity whose active essence stems from that letting belong together which we call the appropriation. The essence of identity is a property of the event of appropriation' (M. Heidegger, *Gesamtausgabe*, Frankfurt am Main: Vittorio Klostermann, 1975 ff; vol. 11, pp. 47–8 [GA]; *Identity and Difference*, edited by J. Staumbaug, New York: Harper & Row, Publishers, 1969, pp. 38–9).

12 Agamben clarifies how the Absolute and the *Ereignis* share the reflexive meaning of the etymological root *se, which both concepts refer to. See G. Agamben, *Potentialities. Collected Essays in Philosophy*, Stanford, CA: Stanford University Press, 1999, pp. 116–37.

13 K. Löwith, *Von Hegel zu Nietzsche. (From Hegel to Nietzsche)*, *Sämtliche Schriften*, 4, Stuttgart: Metzler, 1988, p. 153.

14 GA 45, p. 120.

15 W. Schulz, *Die Vollendung des deutschen Idealismus in der Spätphilosophie Schelling* (1955), (*The Fulfilment of German Idealism in Schelling's Late Philosophy*), Stuttgart: Kohlhammer; Pfullingen: Neske, 1975 (new edn).

16 L. Pareyson, 'Heidegger: la libertà e il nulla' (Heidegger: Freedom and Nothingness), *Annuario Filosofico*, 1989, p. 27.

17 GA 45, p. 184.

18 Ibid.

19 Ibid., p. 185.

20 Ibid., p. 189.

21 Ibid.

22 On the other hand, Heidegger clarifies that technology can certainly decline in the oblivion of being as dominion over the entity, but in actual fact it is other and characterizes the possibility of actively grasping the original *Physis* and 'continuing' it. In the unconcealedness, man does not simply discover himself as *Physis*, but recognizes in himself 'that other that is commensurate with *Physis*, that sets it free and yet understands it' and such other is *Techne*, not the technology as imposition and domination that is at the centre of Heidegger's statement, but rather what that expression meant for the Greeks, namely 'a knowledge: a recognition of being able to proceed in the face of the entity (and in the encounter with the entity), that is to say in the face of the *Physis* […]; a way of proceeding in the face of the *Physis*, not to subdue and exploit it […], but on the contrary to keep *Physis* from imposing itself through the unconcealedness' (GA 45, p. 179).

23 GA 4, p. 56; *Elucidations in Hölderlin's Poetry*, edited by K. Hoeller, New York: Humanity Books, 2000, p. 79.

24 GA 4, p. 59; *Elucidations in Hölderlin's Poetry*, p. 82.

25 Agamben, *Potentialities*, p. 127.
26 GA 14, p. 12; *Time and Being*, edited by J. Macquarrie and E. Robinson, Oxford: Blackwell, 1962, p. 8.

Chapter 1

1 As Francesco Moiso, among others, also notes in his lectures dedicated to Nietzsche (cf. F. Moiso, *Nietzsche e le scienze* (*Nietzsche and the Sciences*), Milan: CUEM, 1999).

2 Compare in particular *Nietzsches persönliche Bibliothek* (*Nietzsche's Personal Library*), edited by G. Campioni, Berlin and New York: De Gruyter, 2002.

3 See also K. Schlechta and A. Anders, *F. Nietzsche, Von den verborgenen Anfängen seines Philosophierens* (*F. Nietzsche, From the Hidden Beginnings of His Philosophy*), Stuttgart: Frommann, 1962.

4 We know how important Ralph Waldo Emerson's essays, which were themselves heavily influenced by Schelling's 'presence', were for Nietzsche already in the early 1860s. In fact, his first philosophical reading concurs precisely with the German translations of *Conduct of Life* and *Essays* by Emerson. In particular, in the essay 'Fate', Emerson highlights the conflict between 'fate' and 'power', evidently imitating Schelling's conflict between 'nature' and 'spirit', and introduces the idea of a coordinated possibility to replace the model of cause and effect. A model that Nietzsche took up as a solution to the problem of Kantian teleology and that later – as I have tried to demonstrate – constituted the dynamic-ontological structure of the Will to Power. Another Schelling source for Nietzsche from 1866 onwards was undoubtedly Friedrich Überweg's book, *Grundriss der Geschichte der Philosophie* (*Sketch of the History of Philosophy*), which contains an entire section dedicated to the life and works of the philosopher from Leonberg.

5 Compare T. H. Brobjer, *Nietzsche's Philosophical Context: An Intellectual Biography*, Urbana and Chicago: University of Illinois, 2008, pp. 60–89.

6 J. E. Wilson, *Schelling Mythologie. Zur Auslegung der Philosophie der Mythologie und der Offenbarung* (*Schelling's Mythology: For an Interpretation of the Philosophy of Mythology and Revelation*), Stuttgart-Bad Cannstadt: Frommann-Holzboog, 1993.

7 In a fragment from 1888 Nietzsche wrote about his departure from Schopenhauer's theses: '(32) DIONYSIAN: a new path to a type of divine, the difference between Schopenhauer and I since the beginning' (F. Nietzsche, *Sämtliche Werke. Kritische Studienausgabe*, edited by G. Colli and M. Montinari, 15 vols, Berlin and New York: De Gruyter, 1967–77 and 1988, vol. XIII, p. 196 [KSA]). Shortly before we read a fundamental passage: 'I understood that my instinct went in the opposite direction to that of Schopenhauer: he tended to justify life, even the most terrible aspects of it. The

formula I had was Dionysian. [...] Schopenhauer did not go so far as to deify the will' (ibid., vol. XII, pp. 354–5).

8 Kant and Plato's readings actually accompany Schelling's and Nietzsche's very first philosophical steps, and in both one can read Kantian criticism in the light of Plato's theories of ideas and vice versa. They are also important for the juxtaposition proposed by the re-evaluation of matter and its active character and the consideration of the Kantian concept of organism, presented by Schelling to the world as *Gesamtorganismus* (total organism) on the basis of the Platonic concept of the world as ζωον νοητον.

9 It should not be forgotten that, as can be seen from the exchange of letters, among other things, it was Jaspers himself who, in the 1920s, encouraged Heidegger to read Schelling's *Philosophical Investigations into the Essence of Human Freedom* (cf. *Martin Heidegger and Karl Jaspers: Briefwechsel 1920-1963*, edited by Walter Biemel and Hans Saner, Frankfurt am Main: Klostermann, 1990).

10 'What is rationally universal is, as such, critical and negative, in other words the intellect itself is destructive; only historicity (*Geschichtlichkeit*) of the irreplaceable, not general, being which rests on itself and is tied to its own grounding, is positive, and which nevertheless remains not only hidden but devoid of essence, if it does not achieve clarity for the intellect. Nietzsche did not have this profound insight, which led Schelling to separate his negative philosophy from his positive philosophy, but he unconsciously followed it' (K. Jaspers, *Nietzsche. Einführung in das Verständinis seines Philosophierens* [*Nietzsche: An Introduction to the Understanding of His Philosophical Activity*], Berlin: Walter de Gruyter, 1950, p. 120).

11 Compare K. Löwith, *Nietzsches Philosophie der ewigen Widerkehr des Gleichen* (*Nietzsche's Philosophy of the Eternal Recurrence of the Same*), Stuttgart: Kohlhammer, 1935.

12 Löwith claims 'Schelling is the only thinker of German idealism who, despite his theogonic constructions, is in a positive relationship with Nietzsche's doctrine of eternal circularity. In the introduction to *The Ages of the World* he says "the living being of supreme science" can only be the "primordial living being", the original and primeval being which has nothing that precedes it and nothing else outside itself, and which consequently *must develop purely from itself, in the most spontaneous way and of its own will* [...]. *As a totally original being it is an In-itself-completed and all-round, concluded and finished, which contains within itself, in equal measure, the original force that destroys and creates. The 'first nature' is a continuous cycle, a rotating movement without rest, without beginning and without end. The original being wants nothing but itself, it is a wanting-itself'* (cf. K. Löwith, *Nietzsches Philosophie der ewigen Widerkehr des Gleichen*, pp. 151–2).

13 G. Lukács, *Die Zerstörung der Vernunft* (*The Destruction of Reason*), Berlin: Aufbau-Verlag, 1954, p. 9.

14 *Heideggers Schelling-Seminar (1927–28) Die Protokolle von Martin Heideggers Seminar zu Schellings „Freiheitsschrift" (1927–28) und die Akten des Internationalen*

Schelling-Tags 2006, edited by L. Hühn and J. Jantzen, Stuttgart-Bad Cannstatt: Frommann-Holzboog, 2010 [HSS].

15 The 1936 lectures, transcribed and integrated in such a way as to give continuity to the text, were published in 1971 by H. Feick in the work entitled *Schellings Abhandlung über das Wesen der menschlichen Freiheit* (*Schelling's Treatise on the Essence of Human Freedom*), Tübingen: Niemeyer [Heidegger 1971], which contains in its appendix some preparatory notes for the 1941–3 courses.

16 'For Nietzsche, the claim that the intimate nature of being is the becoming, in the form of the will to power, and thus of the will to illusion and to fiction, is in its turn a form of the Will to Power, but which is not the will to illusion and to fiction, but the will to truth – the will to truth of the *Übermensch*, that is the 'true doctrine of the will and freedom' taught by Zarathustra' (E. Severino, *L'anello del ritorno* (*The Ring of Recurrence*), Milan: Adelphi, 1999, p. 96).

17 G. Abel, *Nietzsche. Die Dynamik der Willen zur Macht* (*The Dynamics of the Will to Power*), Berlin and New York: De Gruyter, 1998; cf. in particular W. Müller-Lauter, *Über Freiheit und Chaos* (*About Freedom and Chaos*), in *Nietzsche-Interpretationen*, 3 vols, Berlin: De Gruyter, 1999, vol. II.

18 GA, 5, pp. 278–9.

19 F. W. J. Schelling, *Initia philosophiae universae. Erlanger Vorlesung 1820-1821*, edited by H. Fuhrmans, Bonn: Bouvier, 1969, pp. 26–7 [Schelling 1969].

20 Heidegger 1971, p. 4.

21 Ibid., p. 133.

22 KSA, XII, p. 4.

23 Ibid., p. 189.

24 KSA, VII, pp. 428–9.

25 KSA, III, p. 474.

26 It should not be forgotten that already in the early years of the philosophy of Nature, in the 1796–7 *Abhandlungen zur Erläuterung des Idealismus der Wissenschaftslehre* (*Treatises for an Explanation of the Idealism of Science*), Schelling proposes freedom as the common principle in theoretical philosophy and moral philosophy, although, as is evident in such a context, Schelling's freedom does not yet have the ontological character that it later assumed in *Philosophical Investigations*.

27 SW I/7, p. 360.

28 GA 14, pp. 9–10; *On Time and Being*, p. 6.

Chapter 2

1. K. Löwith, *Von Hegel zu Nietzsche* (*From Hegel to Nietzsche*), in *Sämmtliche Schriften*, edited by Klaus Stichweh, Marc B. de Launay, Bernd Lutz and Henning Ritter, 9 Voll., Stuttgart: Metzler, 1981–1988, vol. 4, 1988, pp. 177 ff.

2. Ibid., p. 181.

3. Ibid., p. 153.

4. Ibid., pp. 153–4.

5. SW, II/3, pp. 162–3.

6. Ibid., pp. 165–6.

7. Although Heidegger speaks explicitly about a 'turn' in his thinking in the 1946 *Letter on Humanism* (published the following year), he refers to something that had already happened in his thinking at least a decade earlier (see Richardson, W.J. *Heidegger: From Phenomenology to Thought*. Preface by Martin Heidegger. Collection Phenomenologica, 13, The Hague, Martinus Nijhoff, 1963), that is to say in the mid-1930s in works dating back to that period, such as *Contributions to Philosophy*, *Basic Questions of Philosophy* and *Introduction to Metaphysics*, not forgetting the 1936 course dedicated to Schelling and the lessons dedicated to Nietzsche's philosophy from 1936 to 1940. It has been observed, however, that the reasons for this 'turn' were in part already contained in the provisional conclusions of *Being and Time* and in the need to complete the ontological theses of that work with particular reference to the temporality of being (for a reconstruction of the phases of the 'turn' see M. Ferraris, 'Cronistoria di una svolta (Chronicle of a Turn)', in M. Heidegger, *La svolta* (*The Turn*), edited by M. Ferraris, Italian edn, Genoa: il Melangolo, 1990).

8. Ferraris, *Cronistoria di una svolta* (*Chronicle of a Turn*), pp. 37–122.

9. Martin Heidegger, *Sein und Zeit* (1927); *Being and Time*, English translation edited by J. Macquarrie and J. Robinson, Oxford: Blackwell, 1962, § 8 [SZ].

10. 'All *explicata* to which the analytic of *Dasein* gives rise are obtained by considering *Dasein*'s existence-structure. Because *Dasein*'s characters of Being are defined in terms of existentiality, we call them "*existentialia*". These are to be sharply distinguished from what we call "*categories*" – characteristics of Being for entities whose character is not that of *Dasein*' (SZ § 9).

11. SZ § 29.

12. SZ § 27.

13. HSS, pp. 289–97.

14. SW I/7, p. 381.

15. Pareyson, *Ontologia della libertà* (*Ontology of Freedom*), p. 9.

16. SZ § 39.

NOTES

17 Heidegger 1971, pp. 182 ff.
18 SZ § 40.
19 Ibid.
20 GA 9, p. 113; *Pathmarks*, edited by W. McNeill, Cambridge: Cambridge University Press, 1998, p. 90.
21 Ibid.
22 Ibid.
23 Cf. GA 49, pp. 75 ff.
24 Cf. Ibid., pp. 89 ff.
25 M. Heidegger, *Nietzsche*, 1961, Pfullingen: Verlag Günther Neske, II Band, p. 426 [Heidegger 1961].
26 Heidegger 1961, II, p. 436.
27 In the 1936 *Vorlesung* the term 'Un-grund' is mentioned only once (Heidegger 1971, p. 147) and Heidegger prefers, rather, to speak of absolute Indifference.
28 Heidegger 1971, p. 147.
29 Ibid., p. 148.
30 Ibid.
31 HSS, p. 340.
32 Ibid.
33 Ibid., p. 341.
34 Ibid., p. 342.
35 SW I/7, pp. 365 ff.
36 Heidegger 1971, p. 133.
37 HSS, p. 335.
38 Ibid., p. 344.
39 Ibid., p. 345.
40 Ibid.
41 Ibid., p. 246.
42 SW I/7, p. 385.
43 Heidegger 1971, p. 158.
44 Ibid., p. 157.
45 See SW I/7, p. 350.

Chapter 3

1. Compare GA 15, p. 363.

2. Heidegger traces a complete reconstruction of the 'history of Being' in Volume II of his *Nietzsche*. To summarize the process we can say that Plato's concept, according to which the Being appears as *idea*, or as an intelligible entity whose truth (seen as the revelation-concealing of self) presents itself as the appearance of the Being in the presence, and the Aristotelian concept of Being as *energheia*, as Being in action, that is effectively present (a concept that dominates, according to Heidegger, throughout the Latin Middle Ages in the translation of *actualitas*, and is above all attributed to God) blend together in Descartes's conviction that the true Being has the fundamental characteristic of *certainty*.

   For Descartes, only that which is certain is real and the existence of the *subject* is above all certain. Descartes's diminution of true Being to the certainty of the subject is nothing more than a diminution of things (of entities) to self by the Ego. This diminution is by way of a taking hold, and can be read as the reduction of the Being to the *will* of the subject. Starting from this idea, according to Heidegger, Fichte, Schelling and Hegel built their great philosophical systems which can be summarized in a general diminution of the Being to the will of knowing, of representing – a diminution that led to Nietzsche's Will to Power.

3. Heidegger 1971, p. 231.

4. See Bret W. Davis, *Heidegger and the Will. On the Way to Gelassenheit*, Evanston: Northwestern University Press, 2007, pp. 117 ff.

5. See Heidegger 1971, p. 4.

6. 'Theo-logy' generally means asking the original question about Being in its totality and it has always been the essence and the proceeding of philosophy: philosophy is indeed onto-theo-logy since every philosophy is theo-logy, in the original sense that the conceptual understanding (logos) of the Being as a whole poses the question of the grounding of Being and this grounding (Grund) is called (Theos) God (see Heidegger 1971, p. 98).

7. See H.-J. Friedrich, *Der Ungrund der Freiheit im Denken von Böhme, Schelling und Heidegger* (*The Non-grounding of Freedom in Böhme, Schelling and Heidegger's Thinking*), Stuttgart-Bad Cannstatt: Frommann-Holzboog, 2009, pp. 1–34 and 45–60.

8. GA 79, p. 90.

9. SW I/7, pp. 359–60.

10. Compare M. Gabriel, 'Unvordenkliches Seyn und Ereignis', in *Heideggers Schelling Seminare (1927/28)*, edited by L. Huehn and J. Janzen, Stuttgart-Bad Cannstatt: Frommann-Holzboog, 2010, pp. 81–112 [HSS].

11. Regarding Heidegger on Hegel's Absolute and a confrontation with Agamben's exposition, see the Introduction.

12 Since this would mean introducing a grounding and therefore thinking again within an onto-theological view.

13 Heidegger 1971, p. 231.

14 'The potencies therefore only give themselves within the sphere of appearances, of the phenomena; and the differences in the potencies are mere differences of a quantitative nature, not of Essence (*Wesen*) of the relation itself; the Absolute itself is beyond any potency' (SW I/6, pp. 211 ff., § 58 ff.) (M. Frank, *Natura e Spirito. Lezioni sulla filosofia di Schelling* [*Nature and Spirit. Lessons about Schelling's Philosophy*], Turin: Rosenberg & Sellier, 2010, p. 238).

15 In fact, in the perspective that we propose following Schelling, the idea of totality is impossible, since the Absolute, considered ontologically, is not simply the totality of the existent, but rather an elusive dynamics that, in essential unity with its abyssal Principle, maintains an intimate and coessential relation with Nothingness, that is with that which is not and *must not be* the existent.

16 Again, in *Formschrift* (*On the Possibility of a Form of Philosophy in General*) (1794) and in *Of the I as Principle of Philosophy* (1795) Schelling continues to find in the Kantian categories of *Critique of Pure Reason* (*Kritik der reinen Vernunft*) the principle for their overall deduction, while already in the *Abhandlungen* (*Treatises*) of 1796/97 he sees in *freedom* the possible starting point both for theoretical philosophy and for moral philosophy.

17 GA 11, pp. 45–6; *Identity and Difference*, pp. 36–7.

18 The notion of Ereignis constantly accompanies Heidegger's philosophical production after the 1930s, in particular there are definitions and insights into the concept in *Beiträge für Philosophie* (*Contributions to Philosophy*) [GA 65] as well as in *Besinnung* (*Mindfullness*) [GA 66], *Die Überwindung der Metaphysik* (*On the Overcoming of Metaphysics*) [GA 67], *Die Geschichte des Seins* (*The History of Being*) [GA 69], *Über den Anfang* (*On the Beginning*) [GA 70], *Das Ereignis* (*The Event*) [GA 71] and in the essays collected in *Wegmarken* (*Pathmarks*) [GA 9].

19 GA 9, p. 188; *Pathmarks*, edited by W. McNeill, Cambridge: Cambridge University Press, 1998, p. 144.

20 GA 9, 189; *Pathmarks*, p. 145.

21 Ibid.

22 On this subject, see E. C. Corriero, 'Pensare la natura. La Naturphilosophie di Schelling alla luce della sua filosofia positiva (Thinking about Nature: Schelling's Naturphilosophie in the Light of His Positive Philosophy)', in *Annuario filosofico*, 30, 2015, pp. 171–93.

23 SW I/4, p. 345.

> 'What was held back in prolonged hesitation
> Is here held fast hinting
> As the "level" used for giving it shape.'

25 GA 65, pp. 7–8; *Contributions to Philosophy*, edited by P. Emad and K. Maly, Bloomington: Indiana University Press, 2000, p. 6.

26 GA 65, p. 8; *Contributions to Philosophy*, p. 6.

27 The reference to the few ready for the leap into the other beginning rather explicitly recalls the overcoming desired by Nietzsche in accepting the gift of wisdom of the *Übermensch*.

28 *Contributions to Philosophy* presents precisely six escapes within which the following discourses are articulated: Echo, Playing-Forth, Leap, Grounding, The Ones to Come, The Last God.

29 On the continuity between Schelling's philosophy of nature and his positive philosophy, I refer you to my book, *The Ungrounded Nature of Being*.

30 SW I/3, p. 5.

31 GA 65, p. 11; *Contributions to Philosophy*, p. 9.

32 Cf. GA 49.

33 GA 65, p. 20; *Contributions to Philosophy*, p. 15.

34 Ibid.

35 GA 65, p. 34; *Contributions to Philosophy*, p. 24.

36 GA 65, p. 30; *Contributions to Philosophy*, p. 22.

37 GA 14, pp. 9 ff.; *On Time and Being*, p. 6.

38 GA 14, p. 22; *On Time and Being*, p. 17.

39 GA 14, p. 24; *On Time and Being*, p. 19.

40 Ibid.

41 SW II/3, p. 337.

Chapter 4

1 GA 9, p. 316; *Pathmarks*, pp. 241–2.

2 F. W. J. Schelling, *Philosophie der Offenbarung* (*Philospophy of Revelation*), edited by M. Frank, Frankfurt am Main: Suhrkamp, 1993, p. 165 [Schelling 1993]; emphasis in original.

3 On this question, see the fragment *Urtheil und Seyn* and in particular the comment in Henrich 1991, pp. 55–80; cf. also Frank 2010, pp. 95 ff.

4 In this fundamental aspect, we note an extraordinary affinity with Nietzschean 'ontology' and the becoming, or the *dynamic*, that *commands* it.

5 GA 9, pp. 316 ff.; *Pathmarks*, p. 242.

6 In particular in *Abhandlungen zur Erläuterung des Idealismus der Wissenschaftslehre* (*Treatises for an Explanation of the Idealism of the Science of Knowledge*), written between 1796 and 1797 we can see considerably in advance the development that would then mature in *Philosophical Investigations*, since it supported and overlaid real activity (placed in a priority position with respect to the ideal activity) with a 'true will' as the source of self-consciousness.

7 SW I/4, p. 145.

8 In particular, Frank refers to aphorism XXXIV in *Aphorisms on the Philosophy of Nature* which we partially quote: 'The difficulty most philosophers find in perceiving the unity of the infinite with the finite, or that that is immediately this, derives from their lack of understanding of the absolute identity [...]. In the theory A *is* B, nothing is stated other than that A is the *esse* (the essence) of B (which, for this reason is *not* therefore for itself; but *is* thanks to the link with A). This is precisely the sense of the proposition: *God is in all things*; which in Latin should be expressed not as *Deus est res cuntae*, but rather (*invita latinitate*) as *Deus est res cunctas*. (How things are elevated from the passive to the active, is shown by comparing aphorism VII with aphorism XX)' (SW I/7, p. 205).

9 SW II/3, p. 355.

10 Met. VI, 2, 1026b–1027a; *The Works of Aristotle*, vol. VIII *Metaphysica*, edited by W. D. Ross. Oxford: Clarendon Press, second edition 1928.

11 SW II/4, p. 338.

12 SW I/3, p. 101.

13 Ibid.

14 SW II/2, p. 104.

15 Ibid., p. 105.

16 SW II/3, p. 338.

17 Ibid., pp. 339 ff.

18 Ibid., p. 344.

19 Ibid., p. 347.

20 SW II/2, p. 218.

21 Ibid., p. 219.

22 Ibid., p. 221; emphases in original.

23 SW I/3, p. 345; emphasis in original.

24 *Met.* VI, 2, 1027a.

25 As already mentioned and as we will see in more detail, nonetheless, the contingent of the *unvordenkliches Seyn*, inasmuch as it is 'purely', has to do with the Nothingness seen as οὐκ ὄν.

26 Schelling himself defines, in *Further Presentations from the System of Knowledge*, the meaning of 'speculation': 'the expression [...] should be absolutely reserved to positive philosophy; not even the elementary matesi, for example, can be called speculative: speculative matesi is the highest. "To speculate" means going in search of possibility that allows a given purpose, in science, to be reached. They are certainly only possibilities, which must be demonstrated, later, as reality; just as, in a deduction, what is in the first proposition a hypothesis, in the conclusion is a demonstrated truth' (SW II/3, pp. 344 ff.).

27 Schelling 1993, p. 169.

28 'Contingent is also the not-willed' (Schelling 1993, p. 167) that is that which is blind, that which is casual inasmuch as it is not preceded by a will: 'If I have chosen between +a and –a and I have decided for +a, then –a is excluded for ever; my being +a is not blind: by blind we always and necessary mean a casual being [the cause of which is contingent] while that +a is not something contingent, because it was willed' (SW II/3, p. 338).

Chapter 5

1 L. Pareyson, 'Heidegger: la libertà e il nulla (Heidegger: Freedom and Nothingness)', *Annuario Filosofico*, 5, 1989, pp. 9–29.

2 Ibid., p. 10.

3 GA 9, pp. 111 ff.; *Pathmarks*, p. 88.

4 SW II/3, pp. 162 and 227–9; Schelling states that '"is" has a similar structure to the German *kann* and in Arabic would sound like *kan* and in Hebrew *kun*' (SW I/10, p. 265).

5 Schelling 1993, p. 165.

6 M. Frank, *Natura e Spirito. Lezioni sulla filosofia di Schelling* (*Nature and Spirit. Lessons about Schelling's Philosophy*), Turin: Rosenberg & Sellier, 2010, pp. 287 ff.

7 SW I/6, p. 147.

8 Cf. Ibid., pp. 95 ff.

9 Cf. HSS, p. 324.

10 GA 88, p. 138.

11 In *Vertigini della ragione*, I already emphasized that in the ontological excess shown by Schelling as an absolutely free Principle laid the possibility of reading the Leonberg-born philosopher (and with it also Nietzsche) as post-Heideggerian thinking: The *false unity* through which freedom was harnessed in the *Wissen* and which for Schelling represents the Hegelian experiment intended to enclose reality within the *circle* of rationality, corresponds to the Nietzschean perspective of the Apollonian Will to Power which, in the attempt to include freedom within its interpretation, discovers that knowledge does not know how to go beyond itself and must therefore yield to a *new beginning*, which is discovered in the abyssal and Dionysian basis of the existent: in the eternal *Macht* of the *Wille*, in the eternal *power of the will*.

The hidden danger of the *false unity* is the ever-looming danger of nihilism, a risk that Schelling accepts and overcomes by placing eternal freedom at the basis of the becoming Absolute. Schelling, having discovered the falsity and the limits of the logical foundation, welcomes *ante litteram* the announcement of the 'death of God' and the Heideggerian reading of this event, renouncing the position of a stable and definitive *Grund* in favour of an elusive and unlimited freedom.

In this sense it is possible to understand the definition suggested by Luigi Pareyson of Schelling as a *post-Heideggerian thinker*: although I suggest we should also include Nietzsche, precisely thanks to that affinity with Schelling that I have emphasized in these pages, as a *post-Heideggerian thinker*, in the sense that Nietzsche also overcomes metaphysics and certainly considers the Will to Power as the new *Grund* from which to start again, but not in the *metaphysical, too metaphysical* perspective in which Heidegger means it.' (Corriero 2018a, p. 206).

12 The reflection on φύσις is 'metaphysical' from the beginning in that it concerns the 'set of truths "about" the entity as a whole' (Pathmarks, GA 9, p. 241; trans 185).

13 GA 40, p. 17.

14 GA 9, p. 299; *Pathmarks*, p. 228.

15 GA 4, p. 57; *Elucidations in Hölderlin's Poetry*, p. 80.

16 Ibid., p. 59; *Elucidations in Hölderlin's Poetry*, p. 82.

17 GA 9, p. 301; *Pathmarks*, pp. 229–300.

18 Cf. GA 88, pp. 138 ff.

19 Ibid., p. 143.

20 SW I/10, p. 285.

21 Ibid.

22 Precisely the introduction of this adverb confirms the comparison of the *unvordenkliches Seyn* to the οὐκ ὄν rather than to the μὴ ὄν, with the difficulty that this causes within Schelling's argument, which apparently verges on the alogical, but appears to be the only logical solution destined to 'save' the absolute position of the *unprethinkable being* from an onto-theological reading, and thus guarantee the possibility of absolute Freedom.

23 It is evident that in this context the current Being is not the act of being in power, but rather the absolute *Wirklichkeit* (Reality) as *potentia potentiae*.

24 Schelling 1969, p. 16.

25 Ibid., p. 17.

26 Since – as we have seen – the free decision of being with respect to contrast occurs outside time as succession (*Settelzeit*), that is, in eternity.

27 Schelling 1969, p. 68.

28 Ibid., pp. 24 ff.

29 Freedom is '(a) equal to the eternal, pure potency (*Können*). But also every potency is a knowledge, even though the opposite is not true. (b) Potency in efficiency is will; before passing to efficiency it is will in quiet, will inasmuch as it does not want, indifference' (Schelling 1969, pp. 23 ff.).

30 'It is important not to confuse the Absolute – as absolute subject – with God himself [...] The Absolute is above God' (Schelling 1969, p. 18).

31 Schelling states that every potency is a knowledge (but not vice versa) and that potency in efficiency is will: nonetheless, before moving to the efficiency of the power it is tranquil will, as *not wanting*: indifference.

32 Schelling 1969, p. 25.

33 In the lessons of the philosophy of Revelation, Schelling repeats this relation to Nothingness: 'Brought back to itself [through the relationship with the being] the potency to be appears in the not being, that is with respect to the being, it is the not externally being (*äusserlich*). But precisely inasmuch as it feels itself as Nothingness (that is as a Nothingness, as that total lack of external being) it is like the magic of this Nothingness (the expression *Magie*, 'magic' is one with the German words *Macht* "power" and *Möglichkeit*, "possibility" and therefore equal to "power"). Since this is Nothingness, the potency to be is magic, it is the power that draws into itself the infinitely being, so that, without having to welcome a being, it commands itself in the purely existent as in another self – not as existent, but precisely as infinitely existent. The potency to be must precisely be Nothingness, so that the existent in an infinite, overflowing way becomes something for it' (SW II/2, pp. 231 ff.).

34 Compare Frank 2010, p. 288.

35 Heidegger 1971, p. 95.

36 SW II/2, pp. 128 ff.

37 GA 88, p. 138.

38 Schelling further clarifies this concept and its relation to Nothingness, once again making use of the Aristotelian contingent: the essence of the power of being 'is to be frank, power of being, not however to be existent, but precisely to be potency to be. According to its essence, inasmuch as it subsists as essence, it is the power of

intransitive permanent being in itself. From this intransitive, however, the transitive is only-to-not-exclude itself: and, to the extent to which it is not willed, it is accidental' (SW II/2, p. 230).

39 Since, as we have seen, ontology has always preceded epistemology according to Schelling.

40 Compare SW II/3, pp. 344 ff.

41 Schelling 1969, p. 18.

42 Heidegger 1971, p. 61.

43 About pantheism and freedom in Schelling's *Philosophical Investigations* see E. C. Corriero, *Libertas sive natura. Etica come ontologia in Schelling* (*Libertas sive natura. Ethics as Ontology in Schelling*), in E. C. Corriero (ed), *Libertà e natura. Prospettive schellinghiane* (*Liberty and Nature. Schellingian Perspectives*), Turin: Rosenberg & Sellier, 2017, pp. 65–89.

44 GA 11, p. 79; *Identity and Difference*, edited by J. Stambaugh, New York: Harper & Row, 1969, p. 73.

45 F. Nietzsche, *Der Wille zur Macht* (*The Will to Power*), paragraph 517.

46 'That difficulty lies in language. Our Western languages are languages of metaphysical thinking, each in its own way. It must remain an open question whether the nature of Western languages is in itself marked with the exclusive brand of metaphysics, and thus marked permanently by onto-theo-logic, or whether these languages offer other possibilities of utterance – and that means at the same time of a telling silence' (GA 11, p. 79; *Identity and Difference*, p. 73).

47 GA, 11, p. 70 ff.; *Identity and Difference*, p. 64.

48 GA, 11, p. 71; *Identity and Difference*, p. 65.

49 GA, 11, p. 75; *Identity and Difference*, p. 69.

50 'The negative force (*verneinende*) is for the true essence, or for the existent, the *being*, nonetheless, according to the concept it cannot be identical to the existent and, according to its nature (since it is its opposite), it is the not-being, and therefore in no case the Nothingness (as according to the incorrect translation from the Greek οὐκ ὄν, starting from which the concept of the creation from Nothingness seems to have derived): in fact, how could Nothingness be that which is both being and the force of being itself?' (Schelling 1946, p. 141). This quotation, often used to exclude the idea that Schelling uses οὐκ ὄν in his explanation of the Beginning in relation to absolute Freedom, nevertheless still takes into account the sphere of the manifestation of the Absolute and not the purity of the Absolute *par excellence*. When, in the *Weltalter*, Schelling excludes that we should speak of an οὐκ ὄν, he is still trapped in the coils of metaphysical thinking which prevent him from thinking the Beginning in an absolutely free way; this can still be seen in a problematic way in the *Darstellung des philosophischen Empirismus* (1836). As I have already said, in the Berlin lectures, Schelling tries to resolve the coessential relationship with Nothingness, which

matures dramatically throughout his speculation, through the introduction, definable in a speculative way and always and only *a posteriori*, of the *purely* contingent of the *unvordenkliches Seyn*.

51 GA 65, p. 356; *Contributions to Philosophy*, p. 249.

52 A *new beginning* that contemplates mainly the possibility of the *last God*: a God that evidently exceeds the confines of onto-theology. The relation to the 'higher nothingness' (the 'nothingness in God') does not translate into the nihilist statement about the death of God, but rather constructs the presupposition for the manifestation of God himself, 'the last God is not the end, but the other beginning of immeasurable possibilities in our history [...] The greatest nearness of the last God occurs therefore when the event, inasmuch as it is lingering negation of self, is intensified in the *not-granting* [*refusal*]. This is something essentially other than mere absence. Not-granting as belonging to the event can be experimented only on the more originary essential sway of being, as it lights up in the thinking of the other beginning' (GA 65, p. 411; *Contributions to Philosophy*, p. 289).

BIBLIOGRAPHY

Abel, G. *Nietzsche. Die Dynamik der Willen zur Macht.* Berlin and New York: Walter de Gruyter, 1998

Agamben, G. *Potentialities. Collected Essays in Philosophy.* Stanford, CA: Stanford University Press, 1999.

Aristotle. *The Complete Works of Aristotle: The Revised Oxford Translation.* Ed. J. Barnes. 2 vols. Princeton: Princeton University Press, 1971.

Badiou, A. *Being and Event.* Trans. Oliver Fetham. New York and London: Continuum, 2007.

Biemel, W. and Saner, H. (eds). *Martin Heidegger and Karl Jaspers: Briefwechsel 1920-1963.* Frankfurt am Main: Klostermann, 1990.

Blattner, W. *Heidegger's Temporal Idealism.* Cambridge: Cambridge University Press, 1999.

Bowie, A. *Schelling and Modern European Philosophy. An Introduction.* London: Routledge, 1993.

Brobjer, T. H. *Nietzsche's Philosophical Context: An Intellectual Biography.* Urbana and Chicago: University of Illinois, 2008.

Buchheim, T. *Das Prinzip des Grundes und Schellings Weg zur Freiheitsschrift.* In *Schellings Weg zur Freiheitsschrift. Legende und Wirklichkeit. Akten der Fachtagung der Internationalen Schelling-Gesellschaft 1992.* Eds M. Baumgartner and W. G. Jacobs. Stuttgart and Bad Cannstatt: Frommann-Holzboog, 1996, 223-39

Buchheim, T. »Metaphysische Notwendigkeit des Bösen«. Über eine Zweideutigkeit in Heideggers Auslegung der Freiheitsschrift. In *Zeit und Freiheit. Schelling - Schopenhauer - Kierkegaard - Heidegger.* Ed. I. M. Fehér and W. G. Jacobs. Budapest: Éthos Könyvek, 1999, 183-91.

Cacciari, M. 'Sul Presupposto. Schelling e Rosenzweig'. *Aut aut*, 210-11 (1986), 43-65.

Cacciari, M. *Dell'Inizio.* Milano: Adelphi, 1990.

Cacciari, M. *Della cosa ultima.* Milano: Adelphi, 2004.

Campioni, G. (ed.). *Nietzsches persönliche Bibliothek (Nietzsche's Personal Library).* Berlin and New York: De Gruyter, 2002.

Caputo, J. *The Mystical Element in Heidegger's Thought.* Athens: Ohio University Press, 1978.

Clark, J. *The Problem of Fundamental Ontology.* Toronto: Limits Book Co., 1973.

Corriero, E. C. 'Schelling e Nietzsche. Un percorso teoretico'. *Annuario filosofico*, 28 (2012).

Corriero, E. C. *Nietzsche's Death of God and Italian Philosophy.* London and New York: Rowman & Littlefield, 2016.

Corriero, E. C. *Vertigini della ragione. Schelling e Nietzsche.* Pref. di M. Cacciari. Torino: Rosenberg & Sellier, 2018a.

Corriero, E. C. 'The Ungrounded Nature of Being: Grounding a Dynamic Ontology, From Philosophy of Nature to Positive Philosophy'. *Kabiri. The Journal of North American Schelling Society*, 1 (2018b), 17-35.

Corriero, E. C. 'Schelling Again'. *Rivista di Estetica*, 02 (2020).
Courtine. J.-F. 'Anthropologie et anthropomorphisme. Heidegger lecteur de Schelling'. In *Nachdenken über Heidegger. Eine Bestandsaufnahme*. Ed. U. Guzzoni. Hildesheim: Gerstenberg, 1980, 9–35.
Courtine. J.-F. *Extase de la raison. Essai sur Schelling*. Paris: Galilée, 1990.
Courtine. J.-F. 'Métaphysique et ontothéologie'. In *La Métaphysique: son histoire, sa critique, ses enjeux*. Ed. J.-M. Narbonne and L. Langlois. Paris: Presses Université Laval, 1999, 137–57.
Crowe, B. *Heidegger's Religious Origins*. Bloomington: Indiana University Press, 2006.
Davis, B. W. *Heidegger and the Will: On the Way to Gelassenheit*. Evanston: Northwestern University Press, 2007.
Fehér, I. M. and Jacobs, W. G. (eds). *Zeit und Freiheit. Schelling – Schopenhauer – Kierkegaard – Heidegger. Akten der Fachtagung der Internationalen Schelling-Gesellschaft, Budapest, 24. bis 27. April 1997*. Budapest: Éthos Könyvek, 1999.
Ferraris, M. 'Cronistoria di una svolta (Chronicle of a Turn)'. In M. Heidegger, *La svolta (The Turn)*. Ed. M. Ferraris, Italian edn. Genoa: il Melangolo, 1990.
Ferraris, M. *Manifesto of New Realism*. Trans. S. De Sanctis. New York: SUNY Press, 2014a.
Ferraris, M. *Introduction to New Realism*. London and New York: Bloombsbury, 2014b.
Figal G., *Martin Heidegger. Phänomenologie der Freiheit*. Frankfurt am Main: Athenäum, 1988.
Frank, M. *Eine Einführung in Schellings Philosophie*. Frankfurt am Main: Suhrkamp, 1985.
Frank, M. *Der unendliche Mangel an Sein. Schellings Hegelkritik und die Anfänge der Marxschen Dialektik*. München: Wilhelm Fink, 1992.
Frank, M. *Auswege aus dem Deutschen Idealismus*. Frankfurt am Main: Suhrkamp, 2007.
Frank, M. *Natura e Spirito. Lezioni sulla filosofia di Schelling*. Ed. E. C. Corriero. Torino: Rosenberg & Sellier, 2010.
Friedrich, H.-J. *Der Ungrund der Freiheit im Denken von Böhme, Schelling und Heidegger*. Stuttgart and Bad Cannstatt: Frommann-Holzboog, 2009.
Gabriel, M. *Transcendental Ontology. Essays in German Idealism*. New York and London: Bloomsbury, 2011
Gebhard, W. *Nietzsches Totalismus: Philosophie der Natur zwischen Verklärung und Verhängnis*. Berlin and New York: Walter de Gruyter, 1983.
Geboers, T. *Rückkehr zur Erde: Grundriss einer 'Ökologie der Geschichte' im Ausgang von Schelling, Nietzsche und Heidegger*. Würburg: Ergon Verlag, 2012.
Grant, I. H. *Philosophies of Nature after Schelling*, London: Continuum, 2006.
Guzzoni, G. *Denken und Metaphysik*. Bern and München: Francke, 1977.
Habermas, J. *Das Absolute und die Geschichte: Von der Zwiespältigkeit in Schellings Denken*. Bonn: H. Bouvier, 1954.
Habermas, J. *Dialektischer Idealismus im Übergang zum Materialismus – Geschichtsphilosophische Folgerungen aus Schellings Idee einer Contraction Gottes*. Frankfurt am Main: Suhrkamp, 1971a, 172–227.
Habermas, J. *Theorie und Praxis*. Frankfurt am Main: Suhrkamp Verlag, 1971b.
Halfwassen, J. *Die Bestimmung des Menschen in Schellings Freiheitsschrift*. In *Aktive Gelassenheit. Festschrift für Heinrich Beck zum 70. Geburtstag*. Eds E. Kim, E. Stadel and U. Voigt. Frankfurt am Main: P. Lang, 1999, 503–15.

Heidegger, M. *Nietzsche*. 2 voll. Pfullingen: Neske, 1961.
Heidegger, M. *On Time and Being*. Eds J. Macquarrie and E. Robinson. Oxford: Blackwell, 1962.
Heidegger, M. *Schellings Abhandlung über das Wesen der menschlichen Freiheit*. Ed. H. Feick. Tübingen: Max Niemeyer, 1971.
Heidegger, M. *Gesamtausgabe*. Frankfurt am Main: Klostermann, 1975ff. [GA].
Heidegger, M. *Being and Time*. Trans. J. Macquarrie and E. Robinson. Malden: Blackwell, 1978.
Heidegger, M. *Schelling's Treatise on the Essence of Human Freedom*. Trans. J. Stabaugh. Athens, OH: Ohio University Press, 1985.
Heidegger, M. *Pathmarks*. Ed. W. McNeill. Cambridge: Cambridge University Press, 1998.
Heidegger, M. *Contributions to Philosophy (from Enowning)*. Trans. P. Enad and K. Maly. Bloomington: Indiana University Press, 2000a.
Heidegger, M. *Introduction to Metaphysics*. Trans. G. Fried and R. Polt. New Haven: Yale Nota Bene, 2000b.
Heidegger, M. *Elucidations in Hölderlin's Poetry*. Ed. K. Hoeller. New York: Humanity Books, 2000c.
Heidegger, M. *Heideggers Schelling-Seminar (1927/8). Die Protokolle von Martin Heideggers Seminar zu Schellings „Freiheitsschrift" (1927/8) und die Akten des Internationalen Schelling-Tags 2006*. Ed. L. Hühn e Jörg Jantzen. Stuttgart and Bad Cannstatt: Frommann-Holzboog, 2010 [HSS].
Heinrich, D. *Selbstverhältnisse. Gedanken und Auslegungen zu den Grundlagen der klassischen deutschen Philosophie*. Stuttgart: Reclam, 1982.
Heinrich, D. *Schelling. Größe und Verhängnis*. München: Piper, 1986.
Heinrich, D. *Konstellationen. Probleme und Debatten am Ursprung der idealistischen Philosophie (1789-1795)*. Stuttgart: Klett-Cotta, 1991.
Heinrich, D. *Der Grund im Bewußtsein. Untersuchungen zu Hölderlins Denken (1794-1795)*. Stuttgart: Klett-Cotta, 1992.
Heinrich, D. *Grundlegung aus dem Ich. Untersuchungen zur Vorgeschichte des Idealismus Tübingen - Jena (1790-1794)*. Frankfurt am Main: Suhrkamp, 2004.
Hogrebe, W. *Prädikation und Genesis. Metaphysik als Fundamentalheuristik im Ausgang von Schellings "Die Weltalter"*. Frankfurt am Main: Suhrkamp, 1989.
Holz, H. *Spekulation und Faktizität. Zum Freiheitsbegriff des mittleren und späten Schelling*. Bonn: Bouvier, 1970.
Jantzen, J. and Oesterreich P. L. (eds). *Schellings philosophische Anthropologie*. Stuttgart and Bad Cannstatt: Frommann-Holzboog, 2002.
Jaspers, K. *Nietzsche, Einführung in das Verständnis seines Philosophierens*. Berlin: de Gruyter, 1936.
Kisiel, T. *The Genesis of Heidegger's Being and Time* Berkeley: University of California, 1995
Köhler, D. 'Von Schelling zu Hitler? Anmerkungen zu Heideggers Schelling-Interpretation von 1936 und 1941'. In *Zeit und Freiheit. Schelling - Schopenhauer - Kierkegaard - Heidegger*. Eds. I. M. Fehér and W. G. Jacobs. Budapest: Éthos Könyvek, 1999, 201-13.
Krell, D. F. 'The Crisis of Reason in the Nineteenth Century: Schelling's Treatise »On Human Freedom« (1809)'. In *The Collegium Phaenomenologicum: The First Ten Years*. Ed. J. C. Sallis. Dordrecht: Martinus Nijhoff, 1988, 13-32.

Löwith, K. *Nietzsches Philosophie der ewigen Wiederkehr des Gleichen*. Stuttgart: Kohlhammer, 1935.

Löwith, K. *Von Hegel zu Nietzsche. Der revolutionäre Bruch im Denken des neunzehnten Jahrhunderts*. Stuttgart: Metzler, 1954.

Lukács, G. *Die Zerstörung der Vernunft. Der Weg des Irrationalismus von Schelling zu Hitler*. Berlin: Aufbau-Verlag, 1954.

Marx, W. *Heidegger und die Tradition: Eine problemgeschichtliche Einführung in die Grundbestimmungen des Seins*. Hamburg: Meiner, 1980.

Marx, W. 'Bemerkungen zum Verhältnis von Philosophie und Dichtung bei Schelling und Heidegger'. In *Philosophie und Poesie. Otto Pöggeler zum 60. Geburtstag*. Ed. A. Gethmann-Siefert, vol. 2. Stuttgart and -Bad Cannstadt: Frommann-Holzboog, 1988, 125–41.

Mellaissoux, Q. *After Finitude. An Essay on the Necessity of Contingency*. Trans. R. Brassier. New York and London: Continuum, 2008.

Moiso, F. *Nietzsche e le scienze*. Milan: CUEM, 1999.

Müller-Lauter, W. *Nietzsche. Seine Philosophie der Gegensätze und die Gegensätze seiner Philosophie*. Berlin and New York: de Gruyter, 1971

Müller-Lauter, W. *Über Freiheit und Chaos in Nietzsche-Intrpretationen*, 3 voll. vol. II. Berlin: de Gruyter, 1999.

Nietzsche, F. *Sämtliche Werke. Kritische Studienausgabe*. Ed. G. Colli - M. Montinari, 15 voll. Berlin and New York: Walter de Gruyter, 1967–77, e1988 [KSA].

Norman, J. and Welchman, A. (eds). *The New Schelling*. New York: Continuum, 2004.

Osterwald, U. *Die Zweideutigkeit der Freiheit als Resultat der Willensmetaphysik Schellings*. Bielefeld: Pfeffersche Buchhandlung, 1972.

Pareyson, L. *Ontologia della libertà*. Torino: Einaudi, 2000.

Pöggeler, O. *Der Denkweg Martin Heideggers*. Pfullingen: Neske, 1963.

Richardson, W. J. Preface by Martin Heidegger. *Heidegger: From Phenomenology to Thought*. Collection Phenomenologica, 13, The Hague: Martinus Nijhoff, 1963.

Rojas Jiménez, A. *Das Potenzlose: Die Spur Schellings in der Spätphilosophie Heideggers*. Hildesheim: Olms, 2014.

Safranski, R. *Heidegger: Between Good and Evil*. Trans. E. Osers. Cambridge, MA: Harvard University Press, 1998.

Sartre, J.-P. *L'être et le néant. Essai d'ontologie phénoménologique*. Paris: Gallimard, 1943.

Schelling, F. W. J. *Die Weltalter. Urfassungen*. Ed. Manfred Schröter. München: Biederstein & Leibniz, 1946.

Schelling, F. W. J. *Historisch-kritische Ausgabe der Bayerischen Akademie der Wissenschaften*. Ed. Hermann Krings, Hans Michael Baumgartner and Wilhelm G. Jacobs. Stuttgart and Bad Cannstatt: Frommann-Holzboog, 1976, e segg.

Schelling, F. W. J. *Timaeus*. Ed. Hartmut Buchner. Stuttgart and Bad Cannstatt: Frommann-Holzboog, 1994 (*Schellingiana*, vol. 4).

Schelling, F. W. J. *Sämmtliche Werke*. Ed. Karl Friedrich August Schelling, 14 voll. Stuttgart and Augsburg: Cotta, 1856–1861. Anche su CD-Rom. Ed. Elke Hahn, Berlin: Total-Verlag, 1998 [SW].

Schelling, F. W. J. *Zeitschrift für spekulative Physik*. Ed. Manfred Durner, 2 voll. Hamburg: Meiner, 2001.

Schelling, F. W. J. *Weltalter, Weltalter-Fragmente*. Ed. Klaus Grotsch. Stuttgart and Bad Canstatt: Frommann-Holzboog, 2002.

F. W. J. Schelling's lessons

Erhardt W. E. (ed.). *F.W.J. Schelling, Einleitung in die Philosophie (Nachschrift Bekkers von 1830)*. Stuttgart and Bad Cannstatt: Frommann-Holzboog, 1989 [Schelling 1989].
Frank M. (ed.). *F.W.J. Schelling, Philosophie der Offenbarung 1841–1842 (= Paulus-Nachschrift)*. Frankfurt am Main: Suhrkamp, 1977, e1993 [Schelling 1993].
Fuhrmans H. (ed.). *F.W.J. Schelling, Initia philosophiae universae. Erlanger Vorlesung 1820–1821*. Bonn: Bouvier, 1969 [Schelling 1969].
Fuhrmans H. (ed.). *F.W.J. Schelling. Grundlegung der positiven Philosophie. Münchener Vorlesung 1832–1833 (G. Helmes)*. Torino: Bottega d'Erasmo, 1972.
Peetz S. (ed.). *F.W.J. Schelling. System der Weltalter. Münchener Vorlesung 1827–1828 in der Nachschrift von Ernst von Lasaulx*. Frankfurt am Main: Vittorio Klostermann, 1990, e1998.

Schlechta, K.-A. and Anders, A. (ed.). *F. Nietzsche, Von den verborgenen Anfängen seines Philosophierens*. Stuttgart: Frommann, 1962.
Schulz, W. *Die Vollendung des deutschen Idealismus in der Spätphilosophie Schelling*. Stuttgart and Köln: Kohlhammer, 1955; Pfullingen: Neske, 1975.
Severino, E. *La struttura originaria*. Brescia: La Scuola, 1958.
Severino, E. *Destino della necessità*. Milano: Adelphi, 1980.
Severino, E. *L'anello del ritorno*. Milano: Adelphi, 1999.
Tilliette, X. *L'Absolu et la philosophie*. Paris: Libraire philosophique J. Vrin, 1987.
Tilliette, X. *Schelling. Une philosophie en devenir*. Paris: Libraire philosophique J. Vrin, 1992.
Tilliette, X. *Schelling. Biographie*. Paris: Calmann-Lévy, 1999.
Vattimo, G. *Il soggetto e la maschera*. Milano: Bompiani, 1974.
Vattimo, G. *La fine della modernità*. Milano: Garzanti, 1991.
Vattimo, G. *Dialogo con Nietzsche*. Milano: Garzanti, 2000.
Vattimo, G. *Introduzione a Heidegger*. Roma and Bari: Laterza, 2001 (prima edizione 1971)
Vattimo, G. *Della realtà*. Milano: Garzanti, 2012.
Verra, V. 'Heidegger, Schelling e l'idealismo tedesco'. *Archivio di Filosofia* 1 (1974), 51–71.
Vetö M. (ed.). *F.W.J. Schelling. Stuttgarter Privatvorlesungen (Georgii)*. Torino: Bottega d'Erasmo, 1973.
Volpi, F. *Selvaggia chiarezza*. Milano: Adelphi.
Wieland, W. *Schellings Lehre von der Zeit*. Heidelberg: Carl Winter Universitätsverlag, 1956.
Wilson, J. E. *Schelling Mythologie. Zur Auslegung der Philosophie der Mythologie und der Offenbarung*. Stuttgart and Bad Cannstadt: Frommann-Holzboog, 1993.
Wilson, J. E. *Schelling und Nietzsche: Zur Auslegung der fruhen Werke Friedrich Nietzsche*. New York and Berlin: Walter de Gruyter, 1996.

INDEX

Abel, Günther 27
absolute 2–4, 6, 9–13, 16, 21–5, 27–30, 32, 34, 43, 49, 55, 58, 70, 72, 77, 79, 82–3, 86, 88–93, 95, 100–2, 105, 110–11, 129, 131, 133–7, 139, 141–2, 146–8, 153
Agamben, Giorgio 3, 10
   Potentialities 3
ancestrality 3
anxiety 52, 54–8, 66, 75–6, 129–31

Bachofen, Johann Jacob 19
   Gräbersymbolik 19
beginning 5–8, 11–13, 20, 27–8, 34, 49, 59, 62–4, 69, 86, 88, 93, 97–8, 101–2, 107–8, 111, 113–16, 120, 123–4, 128, 135, 139–40, 146, 148–9, 153
being 1–13, 15–16, 23, 25–8, 31–7, 41–50, 52–103, 105–25, 127–43
   being as presence 72, 83, 98, 102, 105, 130, 140
   being-there 40, 42, 50–1, 55–6, 94–5, 99
   Dasein 5–6, 40, 44–7, 50–2, 55, 57, 66, 81, 94, 97–9, 129, 135
   concept of being 33, 41, 68, 72, 78, 82, 107–9
   history of being 7, 13, 20, 28, 36, 46, 58–62, 65–6, 80–3, 86–7, 89, 92, 100–2, 129, 136
   oblivion of being 7–8, 12, 59–61, 64, 82, 99
   original being 16, 22, 31, 49, 59, 63, 68, 73, 75, 84, 86, 106–7
   reserve of being 6, 87, 128–9, 142, 145, 151
   truth of being 5, 63, 81, 88, 94, 96, 99
   unprethinkable being 31, 62, 103, 108–9, 117–20, 125, 134, 143, 145
   unvordenkliches Seyn 13, 63, 88, 108, 110–11, 113–14, 122, 124–5, 129, 133–4, 137, 139, 142, 151
Burckhardt, Jacob 19

contingency 6, 103, 108, 120, 125
   contingent 120, 123–4, 134, 139
copula 11, 72, 110, 112–13, 115, 125, 132–3, 140–9
Creuzer, Friedrich 18
crisis 15, 19, 28, 31–2

De Caro, Mario 1
dynamics 5–7, 13, 22, 26–9, 32, 41, 46, 66, 72, 75, 82–3, 86, 88, 90, 95, 102, 109–10, 113, 118–19, 122, 125, 129, 131, 134–6, 138, 141–2, 145–8, 151–3, notes 163–4

epistemology 146
event 3, 10, 13, 36, 52–3, 55, 58, 85, 88, 93–5, 98–9, 102, 151–2
   Enteignis 3, 95, 137, 151
   Ereignis 2–4, 6–7, 9–13, 35–6, 41, 52–3, 55, 62–3, 82–6, 88–90, 92–103, 105, 108–9, 127, 129–31, 135, 137, 151–3
excess 2–3, 35–6, 84, 86–8, 90, 95, 146, 149, 152
   dynamic excess 8, 10, 146
   ontological excess 2–3, 5–6, 8, 11, 16, 86, 135–6
existence 5–6, 23–4, 39–45, 50, 55, 60, 64, 66, 69–70, 72–4, 76, 87–8, 95, 107, 114–17, 119, 123, 132, 135, 137
   existence of God 107
   philosophy of existence 4–5, 42, 50

INDEX

facticity 52, 95
Ferraris, Maurizio 1
Feuerbach, Ludwig 39–40, 49
force 6, 31–3, 55, 70–1, 74–7, 109–10, 112–15, 120–2, 125, 133, 141
Frank, Manfred 18–19, 44, 107–8, 112, 131, 133, 143
   Der kommende Gott 18
   Gott im Exil 18
freedom 6, 12, 16–17, 20, 26–32, 34–6, 41–2, 44, 46, 48, 50, 54–5, 58, 60, 63–7, 74–6, 78, 80, 82, 83, 85–7, 89, 94–6, 98, 108–9, 114, 116, 118–20, 122, 124–5, 127–9, 131, 134, 137–43, 145–8, 153

Geworfenheit 50
god 9, 18, 22–3, 28–9, 40–6, 69, 70, 73–4, 79, 84, 97–9, 107, 114, 116–18, 136, 144, 147
   godhead 137–8
Grant, Iain Hamilton
   Philosophies of Nature after Schelling 75
grounding 5–7, 9, 16, 21–2, 27–9, 34, 36–7, 41–4, 46, 49–50, 52, 55–6, 58, 60–1, 63–76, 78, 80, 85–7, 89, 92, 94–9, 108, 112–13, 115, 119, 122–3, 125, 129, 132, 134–5, 140, 142, 148–50, 152

Hartmann, Eduard von 20–1
   Philosophy of the Unconscious 20–1
   Schelling's Positive Philosophy as unity of Hegel and Schopenhauer 21
Hartmann, Nicolai 47
Hegel 1–4, 10, 21, 24, 26, 31, 39–42, 44–5, 49, 53–4, 77, 82, 87, 90, 111, 116, 137, 148, 151
Heidegger, Martin 2–8, 9–13, 16–17, 23, 25–7, 29–32, 35, 36, 41–2, 44–85, 87–101, 103, 105–10, 118, 124, 127–31, 134–7, 141, 143–4, 148, 150–3

Being and Time 4–5, 25, 42, 46, 50, 52–3, 57–8, 61, 93, 94–5
Contributions to Philosophy 7, 53, 93, 95–7
Essence of Truth 58, 94–5
Fundamental Questions of Philosophy 7, 48
Identity and Difference 3, 152
Kant and the Problem of Metaphysics 48
Letter on Humanism 4, 12, 82, 105–6, 109
Sein und Zeit 41, 45–8, 50–1, 53–7, 60, 67, 76, 81, 101, 105, 129–31
Time and Being 100
Was ist Metaphysik? 6, 29, 36, 56–7, 64, 105, 124, 127, 130
Herder, Johann Gottfried 18
Hölderlin, Friedrich 2, 8, 18, 133, 136

idealism 1, 15, 17, 24–6, 31, 35, 39, 45, 54, 59–60, 67–8, 77, 80, 82, 84, 86–7, 98, 101, 106, 129, 148
identity 72, 78, 80, 83, 88–9, 110, 112, 120–1, 125, 133, 141–52
   philosophy of identity 9, 26, 41, 70–1, 78–80, 89–90, 105, 110, 111, 113, 120, 133
im-position 92
   Gestell 93, 100
indifference 13, 25, 55, 61, 66, 68–9, 71–3, 75–6, 87, 89, 95, 110–11, 122, 130, 133–4
intellect 6, 16, 33, 36, 65, 69, 82
   intellectual intuition 1, 24

Jaspers, Karl 15, 17, 23, 25, 27, 32, 46, 52, 127
   Nietzsche: An Introduction to the Understanding of His Philosophical Activity 23

Kant, Immanuel 17, 23, 33–4, 40–3, 47, 66, 77, 107–8, 123, 132
   Critique of Judgement 23, 34, 77
   Critique of Pure Reason 59

The Only Possible Argument in Support of a Demonstration of the Existence of God 41
Kein, Otto 17–18, 21
  The Apollonian and Dionysian in Nietzsche and Schelling 17
Kierkegaard, Søren 49–50, 54, 60
  The Concept of Anxiety 54
knowledge 7, 15, 17–18, 20, 23, 25–6, 28, 31–4, 46, 51, 53, 66, 74, 86, 89–92, 103, 116, 131, 140–3, 148–9, 151–2

Leibniz, Gottfried Wilhelm von 66, 80
Lichtung 8–9, 94, 97–8, 136, 152
Löwith, Karl 4–5, 16–17, 23, 27, 32, 34, 39–42, 44–6, 50, 52, 95
  From Hegel to Nietzsche: The Revolution in Nineteenth-Century Thought 40, 45
Lukács, Györky 1, 17, 24
  The Destruction of Reason 24

Meillassoux, Quentin
  Après la finitude 2
Meister Eckhart 52, 66
metaphysics 6–7, 10, 12–13, 16, 25, 36–7, 42, 45, 49, 59, 65, 82, 86–7, 93, 98–100, 129, notes 156, 167, 169
  metaphysics of the will 35, 58, 60, 66, 67–8, 71, 77, 84
  metaphysics of evil 58, 60, 63–4, 67
Mitwissenschaft 52, 98, 129
Mögen 27, 29, 105, 109, 113, 125, 141–2, 149
Müller-Lauter, Wolgang 27
mythology 4, 18–19, 21, 49

nature 1–2, 4, 7, 8, 9
Nichts 6, 29, 36–7, 64, 103, 105
Nietzsche 8, 15–28, 27–36, 39–40, 42–3, 45–6, 48–9, 50, 53, 56, 59–63, 65, 68, 71, 77, 80, 83–6, 87–8, 93, 97, 148–50
  Also sprach Zarathustra 23
  The Gay Science 33, 42

nothingness 6, 26, 29, 36–7, 55, 58, 87, 103, 106, 108, 112, 118, 120–1, 123–4, 127–31, 135–43, 145–6, 148–9, 151–3

Oehlers, Max
  Nietzsches Bibliothek 20
ontology 11, 16, 26, 41, 47, 57, 59, 68, 76–7, 109, 112–13, 122, 129, 131, 134, 136, 143, 145–6
  dynamic ontology 77, 80
onto-theology 11, 16, 84, 86, 92, 102, 129, 134, 138, 147–8
  onto-theological 6, 9, 10, 12–13, 97, 99, 135, 149–50, 152
Overbeck, Franz 19–20

Physis 2, 6–13, 28, 45, 96, 129, 134
Plato 23, 77, 132
potency 12, 27, 90, 116–18, 125
  potency to be 28, 42–3, 51, 57, 119–21, 125, 143, 146, notes 168
  potency to will 27, 106, 141
principle 11–12, 21–2, 24, 31, 34–5, 45, 50, 60, 62, 65, 66, 70, 72, 74, 76, 78–80, 84, 86, 91, 92, 98, 101, 103, 108, 111–12, 115, 118–20, 124–5, 133–44, 146–8

realism 1, 4, 40, 79–80, 86
  new realism 1, 10
  over-realism 1, 88, 125
reason 5–6, 11, 16, 21, 24, 26, 28, 30–2, 35, 39, 42, 43–4, 50, 56, 59, 73, 75, 80, 82–5, 87, 89, 101, 103, 106, 110, 112, 123, 125, 135, 141, 149
revelation 4, 19, 49, 67
  philosophy of revelation 107, 115, 125
Ruge, Arnold 39–40

Schelling 1–6, 9–13, 15–21, 23–36, 39–50, 52–98, 101–3, 105–25, 127–9, 131–53
  Another Deduction of the Principles of Positive Philosophy 92, 102, 117, 137, 139

Aphorisms as an Introduction to the Philosophy of Nature 75
Ideas for a Philosophy of Nature 17
Philosophical Investigations into the Essence of Human Freedom 3, 9–10, 20, 25–6, 29–32, 35, 39, 41, 44, 46, 49, 52–5, 59, 61–9, 73–9, 82, 85, 87, 91, 94–5, 98, 110, 113, 118–19, 122, 124, 131, 143, 147–8
System of Transcendental Idealism 17
Schlegel, August Wilhelm
Lectures on Dramatic Art and Literature 18
Schopenhauer, Arthur 20–2
The World as Will and Representation 22
Schulz, Walter 6, 17, 24–5, 29
The Completion of German Idealism in Schelling's Late Philosophy 24
Spinoza 118
spirit 34, 76, 80, 111, 118

technology 8, 93
totality 7, 9, 16, 31, 34, 42, 51, 55–6, 76, 82, 90–2, 96, 113, 130, 135–6, 141, 149
transcendence 57–8, 130–1

transitive 11, 41, 72, 108, 112, 120, 125, 132–3, 140, 142–5, 147–9
turn 1, 4–7, 23, 34, 44–6, 50, 52–3, 57–8, 63–4, 81, 93–6, 98, 105

Übermensch 19–20, 22–3, 29, 45–6
Ungrund 3, 9–20, 13, 28, 36, 49, 61–3, 65–9, 71–3, 76, 85–9, 92, 95, 108, 110–11, 113–14, 118, 122, 134–35, 139

will 16, 21–3, 25, 26–8, 30, 32–3, 35, 49, 54, 56, 58–71, 73–5, 77, 79–80, 82, 84–7, 91, 94, 99, 120–2, 125, 137
will to love 27, 58, 65, 71, 85
Will to power 20, 22, 26, 28, 30, 32–4, 59, 61–2, 85–6, 148–9
Wille zur Macht 22, 25–7, 29–30, 36, 45, 48, 59–61, 68, 71, 80, 86
Wilson, John Elbert 21–2
Schelling and Nietzsche: On the Interpretation of Nietzsche's Early Works 21
Wirklichkeit 4, 26, 28–9, 31–2, 39–41, 44–5, 49, 59, 61–3, 65, 84, 95, 108, 112, 137, 143, 146
wisdom 28, 33, 141

www.ingramcontent.com/pod-product-compliance
Lightning Source LLC
Chambersburg PA
CBHW052046300426
44117CB00012B/2002